A SALUTE TO WOMEN AND THEIR ZEST FOR FOOD

THE JUNIOR LEAGUE OF WICHITA, KANSAS

First Edition
First Printing, August 1995
20,000 copies

Printed in the U.S.A.
by Rand Graphics, Inc.
Wichita, KS



Library of Congress
Catalog Card Number 95-077531

ISBN 0-9609676-2-1

**CONCEPT & DESIGN:**
Greteman Group
Design for Visual Communication
Wichita, KS 67202

**ILLUSTRATION:**
Sonia Greteman

**COPY CONTRIBUTION:**
Patrick Jennings
Wichita, KS

**FOR ADDITIONAL COPIES, PLEASE CONTACT:**
The Junior League of Wichita, Inc.
6402 East 12th
Wichita, KS 67206
(800) 881 6637

# COOKBOOK COMMITTEE

The Junior League of Wichita gives a tip of the *toque blanche* and a deep bow of sincere appreciation to those members and friends who contributed their recipes and tastebuds to this long-term project. You are the bubbles in our glass, the icing on our cake, the baking powder in our biscuits. We are grateful for your contributions. This book could not have been what it is without you.

## The Steering Committee:

Chairs . . . . . . . . . . Sharol Rasberry, Candace Stultz

Editors . . . . . . . . . . Jerryanne Hadley, Susie Stallings, Ellen Winter

Recipe Doctors . . . . . . . . . . Gretchen Andeel, Kiki Cohlmia, Norma Greever, Nancy Bell Ringer

## Committee Members:

Teresa Boyd
Michelle Breault
Jenny Campbell
Tish Cohlmia
Dolores David
Julie Davis
Luann Delgado
Deb Dennington
Cokie Diggs
Cena Eftekar
Katie Frank
Linda Hill
Susan Holmgren
Mary Jane Kilgore
Clare Korst
Kathy Krumsick
Celeste Lee
Katie Lynn
Sandy Mathiesen
Debbie McCann
Michelle McMillan
Cathy Murphy
Marta O'Neill
Sue Poston
Linda Priest
Joanne Pafume
Ann Patterson
Kathy Pelz
Paige Foust Penner
Polly Prendergast
Sharie Quattlebaum
Terri Ramseyer
Kathy Randall
Roxanne Reber
Sally Rogers
Carrie Spear
Katie Stout
Lynn Tatlock
Joanie Urban
Lise VanArsdale-Hanson
Susan Vetter
Tammi Wallace
Patty West
Christie Wilson
Denise Ziegler

APPETIZERS & BEVERAGES

BREADS & BRUNCHES

SOUPS & SALADS

ENTRÉES

VEGETABLES & SIDE DISHES

MENUS

# TABLE OF CONTENTS

DESSERTS

CARRY NATION

# NATION'S TEMPTATIONS

## "Forget the nachos, bartender, I'll just have a Whiskey Smash."

History tells us that Carry Nation crusaded against Demon Rum. But Kansas culinary legend tells a different story. ❖ Not long after the nineteenth century breathed its last, a prairie twister named Carry bore down on the saloons of Kansas. Sure, she broke bottles and mirrors and hacked up paintings of a nekkid Cleopatra. But what she was really after was the Blue Plate Special. ❖ Carry, you see, was Kansas' first food critic. Here's the way she worked: if she liked the food, the hatchet stayed in her purse. But, if she didn't like the food, watch out. For example, if you used garlic powder instead of fresh garlic: "One Big Hatchet Hack." Vodka in a martini would put the whole saloon in mortal danger. (Carry once told her fellow members of the Women's Culinary Terrorist Unit, "Vodka is for Russians. Gin is for martinis!") So, with Carry's rating system, "No Hacks" would translate into today's five-star food and drink. ❖ Alas and alack, Carry and the WCTU finally realized the tide was against them. Kansans—and all Americans—are an independent lot. If we want to put tequila in a martini, no one's going to stop us. ❖ The following recipes for appetizers and libations may take a few twists on the classics, but surely every one of them would have convinced Carry to bury her hatchet.

# Appetizers & Beverages

SERVINGS
5 cups

# Aegean Salsa

Sauté onion, eggplant, bell peppers, tomatoes, celery and garlic in oil. Cook over low heat for 30 minutes, stirring frequently. Stir in wine, sugar, Worcestershire sauce, salt and pepper and continue cooking for 15 minutes. Add capers and olives then cook an additional 15 minutes. Cool for 30 minutes. Cover and chill for at least 2 hours. Serve with Pita Crisps or toasted pumpernickel.

**1 cup diced onion**
**1 large eggplant, peeled and cut into ½-inch cubes**
**1 green bell pepper, diced**
**1 red bell pepper, diced**
**5 medium tomatoes, peeled, seeded and diced**
**½ cup diced celery**
**1 clove garlic, minced**
**½ cup olive oil**
**½ cup dry white wine**
**1 teaspoon granulated sugar**
**1 teaspoon Worcestershire sauce**
**Salt and freshly ground pepper, to taste**
**2 tablespoons capers**
**1 can (3.8 ounces) sliced black olives, drained**

SERVINGS
48 pieces

# Pita Crisps

Preheat oven to 350 degrees. Cut each pita round into eighths and separate wedges. Place wedges on an ungreased baking sheet. Bake until lightly browned, 10 minutes. Cool on wire racks and store in an airtight container.

**3 whole wheat pita rounds**

SERVINGS
2 cups

# HUMMUS

Microwave garbanzo beans with liquid on high for 5 minutes. Pour off liquid and reserve. Mince garlic in food processor, add salt and beans and pulse 10 times. Add tahini, lemon juice and reserved liquid and process until mixture is consistency of a creamy paste. Spoon into a serving bowl and drizzle with a thin film of olive oil. Garnish with pine nuts and paprika. Serve with pita bread or crudités. Hummus may be refrigerated for several weeks. If it becomes too thick, add a little hot water and stir.

**1 can (15 ounces) garbanzo beans, with liquid**
**1 clove garlic**
**1 teaspoon salt**
**½ cup tahini**
**¼ cup fresh lemon juice**
**Olive oil**
**¼ cup pine nuts, toasted**
**Paprika**

*Tahini is a thick paste made from sesame seed. It is available in specialty food stores. If tahini has separated, pour oil off and reserve. Remove desired amount of tahini, then pour oil back into remaining tahini to maintain freshness.*

It's sad to grow old but nice to ripen.

*Brigitte Bardot*

SERVINGS
40 Pieces

# BAJA NACHOS

Combine cheese, green chilies, olives, onions and mayonnaise in a large bowl. Gently fold in shrimp. Top each chip with a rounded teaspoon of cheese mixture. Microwave nachos on high until cheese is melted, 1 minute. Serve with Salsa Fresca (page 32).

*Nachos may also be broiled in oven. Watch carefully to avoid browning chips.*

**1½ cups (6 ounces) grated cheddar cheese**
**1 can (4½ ounces) chopped green chilies**
**1 can (2¼ ounces) sliced black olives, drained**
**¼ cup sliced green onions**
**¼ cup mayonnaise**
**¼ pound tiny shrimp, cooked**
**40 round tortilla chips**

SERVINGS
3 cups

# CHEESE & ARTICHOKE TORTA

Preheat broiler. Place whole pepper directly on oven rack. Broil until sides start to blister and brown. Immediately remove pepper from oven and place in a paper bag. Close and let stand for 20 minutes. Remove pepper from bag, peel, seed, then chop. Combine chopped pepper, artichokes and parsley and set aside. In a medium bowl beat cream cheese and salad dressing mix until smooth. Line a deep 3-cup bowl with plastic wrap. Divide cheese mixture into thirds and vegetable mixture in half. Alternate layers of cheese and vegetable mixtures, beginning and ending with cheese. Chill for at least 4 hours. Invert on plate, remove plastic wrap and serve with assorted crackers.

**1 medium red bell pepper**
**1 jar (6 ounces) marinated artichoke hearts, drained and chopped**
**3 tablespoons minced fresh parsley**
**2 packages (8 ounces each) cream cheese, softened**
**1 package (1 ounce) ranch-style salad dressing mix**

SERVINGS
32 pieces

# Polenta Triangles with Peppers & Gorgonzola

6½ cups water
2 teaspoons salt
2 cups instant polenta
Extra virgin olive oil
2 large red bell peppers, diced
1 large yellow bell pepper, diced
2 tablespoons extra virgin olive oil
Salt and freshly ground pepper, to taste
4 ounces Gorgonzola cheese, softened

Lightly oil an 8½ x 4½ x 2½-inch loaf pan. In a 3-quart saucepan bring water and salt to a boil. Quickly add polenta in a steady stream, stirring constantly with a wooden spoon. Reduce heat to medium and continue stirring until polenta is thick and smooth, 5 minutes. Pour into prepared pan. Smooth top with a wet spatula and cool. (If making ahead, cover with plastic wrap and chill for up to 24 hours.) Invert polenta and cut into ½-inch slices. Cut each slice diagonally into two triangles. Lightly brush on both sides with olive oil and arrange on a baking sheet. Broil polenta 5 inches from heat for 3 to 5 minutes per side. Triangles will be crisp on outside and flecked with brown.

Sauté bell peppers in oil. Season to taste, cover and cook over medium heat until peppers are tender, about 10 minutes. Top each triangle with 1 tablespoon peppers and ½ teaspoon Gorgonzola cheese. Return triangles to 200 degree oven to warm, but not melt cheese. Serve immediately.

*Polenta is made from cornmeal and may be found in specialty food stores.*

SERVINGS
32 slices

# Rolled Soufflé with Caviar or Smoked Salmon

Preheat oven to 375 degrees. Line a 15½ x 10½ x 1-inch jelly-roll pan with parchment paper. Butter generously, then dust with flour. In a medium saucepan make a thick paste with flour and ¼ cup milk. Stir in remaining milk and cook over medium heat, stirring constantly until mixture thickens. Remove from heat. Beat in egg yolks then add seasonings. Whip egg whites until stiff and fold into milk mixture. Spread evenly into prepared pan. Bake for 20 to 25 minutes. Remove from oven and cover with a damp tea towel. Invert pan and carefully remove paper. Cover soufflé with a clean sheet of paper and roll up in the towel, starting with long side. Chill for at least 2 hours.

Remove soufflé from refrigerator and unroll, removing damp towel and paper. Spread evenly with desired filling. Roll up tightly and cover with plastic wrap. Chill for several hours before serving. With a serrated knife cut into ½-inch slices and serve on a platter garnished with parsley.

Caviar filling: Combine cream cheese, sour cream, onion tops and lemon juice. Rinse caviar and pat dry with paper towels. Fold caviar into cream cheese mixture. Do not chill before spreading on soufflé roll.

Salmon filling: Purée salmon and onion in a food processor. Gradually add butter then sour cream and blend until smooth. Add lemon juice and dill weed. Chill for at least 2 hours before spreading on soufflé roll.

**Soufflé roll:**
- ¼ cup all-purpose flour
- 1 cup milk
- 2 egg yolks
- ¾ teaspoon salt
- ¼ teaspoon white pepper
- ¼ teaspoon ground nutmeg
- 3 egg whites, room temperature
- Fresh parsley sprigs for garnish

**Caviar filling:**
- 1 package (8 ounces) cream cheese, softened
- 3 tablespoons sour cream
- 3 tablespoons sliced green onion tops
- 1 teaspoon fresh lemon juice
- 1 jar (2 ounces) lumpfish caviar

**Salmon filling:**
- 12 ounces smoked salmon
- 1 tablespoon minced onion
- ½ cup butter, melted
- 1 cup sour cream
- 1 tablespoon fresh lemon juice
- 1 teaspoon dried dill weed

SERVINGS
¾ cup

# Gorgonzola Bites

Beat cream cheese, Gorgonzola, horseradish and milk until smooth. Spoon into a pastry bag or decorator tube fitted with star tip. Pipe onto zucchini slices, cucumber slices, celery sticks, carrot sticks or cherry tomatoes and garnish.

1 package (3 ounces) cream cheese, softened
1 ounce Gorgonzola cheese, crumbled
1 tablespoon horseradish
1 tablespoon milk
Assorted vegetables
Fresh parsley, fresh dill or pimiento for garnish

A woman is like a tea bag. You never know how strong she is until she gets in hot water.

*Eleanor Roosevelt*

SERVINGS
20 tomatoes

# BLT Cherry Tomatoes

Cook bacon until crisp. Drain, crumble and set aside. Trim ¼ inch off top of each tomato with a serrated knife. Carefully scoop out seeds and discard. Lightly salt inside of tomato shells and invert on paper towels for 15 minutes. In a small bowl combine onions, bacon, lettuce and mayonnaise. Season with salt and pepper. Fill each tomato with bacon mixture. Cover and chill. Serve on a bed of fresh parsley.

**8 slices bacon**
**20 cherry tomatoes**
**¼ cup thinly sliced green onions**
**½ cup finely chopped romaine lettuce**
**¼ cup mayonnaise**
**Salt and freshly ground pepper, to taste**
**1 bunch fresh parsley for garnish**

SERVINGS
30-40 pieces

# Brie Wafers

Remove rind from cheese and bring to room temperature. Place cheese, butter, flour and seasonings in a food processor and blend until mixture forms a ball. Divide mixture in half and roll each portion into a log 1½ inches in diameter. Brush with egg and roll in walnuts. Cover and chill for at least 2 hours.

Preheat oven to 425 degrees. Line a baking sheet with parchment paper. Cut cheese logs into ¼-inch slices and bake until lightly browned, 12 to 15 minutes.

*Cheese logs may be refrigerated up to one week or wrapped in foil and frozen before baking.*

**8 ounces Brie cheese**
**½ cup butter, softened**
**1¼ cups all-purpose flour**
**1 teaspoon dry mustard**
**¾ teaspoon salt**
**⅛ teaspoon black pepper**
**1 egg, lightly beaten**
**1 cup finely chopped walnuts, toasted**

SERVINGS
25-30 pieces

# ALASKAN SNOW PEAS

Blanch snow peas in boiling, salted water for 10 seconds and immediately rinse in cold water. Drain and set aside. When cool, split on top side, leaving bottom intact to form a boat. Combine remaining ingredients in a medium bowl. Stuff each snow pea with a heaping teaspoon of filling. Chill until ready to serve.

- ½ pound fresh snow peas, strings removed
- 12 ounces cooked, shredded crabmeat
- 2 hard-cooked eggs, finely diced
- ¼ cup mayonnaise
- 3 tablespoons minced celery
- 1 tablespoon fresh lemon juice
- 1 teaspoon capers (optional)
- 2 or 3 dashes hot pepper sauce
- ⅛ teaspoon garlic powder

SERVINGS
36 pieces

# ZUCCHINI PUFFS

Slice zucchini into ¼-inch rounds. In a small bowl combine remaining ingredients. Spread each zucchini slice with a thin layer of mixture. Cover and chill until ready to serve.

Preheat broiler. Arrange zucchini on broiler pan and broil 5 inches from heat until golden brown, 30 to 60 seconds. Serve warm.

- 2 medium zucchini
- ⅓ cup mayonnaise
- ½ cup freshly grated Parmesan cheese
- ½ teaspoon dried basil

# CROSTINI & TOPPINGS

SERVINGS
48 pieces

## CROSTINI

Preheat oven to 400 degrees. Slice bread into ¼-inch rounds. Brush olive oil on both sides of bread slices and arrange on a baking sheet. Toast in oven until bread is light golden and still soft in the center, 1 to 2 minutes on each side. Peel garlic and cut in half. Rub one side of each piece of toast with cut garlic. Serve crostini with assorted toppings.

*Using olive oil spray is an easy way to coat bread. Crostini may be made ahead and stored in an airtight container for several days.*

**1 baguette French bread (2-inch diameter)**
**¼ cup extra virgin olive oil**
**4 cloves garlic**

SERVINGS
2 cups

## AVOCADO & GOAT CHEESE

Mash avocado until smooth. Add remaining ingredients and stir until just combined. Serve at room temperature.

**1 ripe avocado**
**1 package (5½ ounces) goat cheese, softened**
**1 tablespoon fresh lemon juice**
**1 teaspoon extra virgin olive oil**
**Salt and freshly ground pepper, to taste**

SERVINGS
1½ cups

## BELL PEPPER & ONION

Sauté onion in oil and butter until tender, about 5 minutes. Add garlic and sauté another minute. Stir in bell pepper, water and salt. Cover and cook over low heat until pepper is soft, about 30 minutes. Stir occasionally. Serve at room temperature.

**1 medium onion, diced**
**2 tablespoons extra virgin olive oil**
**2 tablespoons unsalted butter**
**2 cloves garlic, minced**
**1 yellow bell pepper, diced**
**¼ cup water**
**⅛ teaspoon salt**

SERVINGS

¾ cup

# TAPENADE

Pulse olives and garlic in food processor until coarsely chopped. Add olive oil and process to make a dense paste. Transfer to a small bowl and stir in capers and lemon zest. Cover and chill overnight. Serve at room temperature.

*May be prepared several days ahead, allowing flavors to blend.*

1 cup imported black olives in brine, pitted
1 clove garlic, minced
1 tablespoon extra virgin olive oil
1 tablespoon capers
2 teaspoons lemon zest

SERVINGS

2 cups

# TOMATO & FETA

Sauté shallots in oil until tender. Stir in tomatoes, salt and pepper. Cook until just heated, 1 minute. In a bowl combine tomato mixture with cheese, chives and vinegar. Serve at room temperature.

2 shallots, thinly sliced
1 tablespoon extra virgin olive oil
4 medium tomatoes, peeled, seeded and diced
Salt and freshly ground pepper, to taste
2 ounces feta cheese, diced
2 tablespoons snipped fresh chives
2 teaspoons balsamic vinegar

SERVINGS

2 cups

# TOMATO & MINT

Toss tomatoes with olive oil, basil, mint and garlic. Season with salt and pepper and let stand for 3 hours at room temperature to allow flavors to blend. Serve at room temperature.

4 medium tomatoes, peeled, seeded and diced
¼ cup extra virgin olive oil
¼ cup minced fresh basil, tightly packed
1½ tablespoons minced fresh mint leaves
1 clove garlic, minced
Salt and freshly ground pepper, to taste

# PHYLLO & PHYLLINGS

SERVINGS
60 triangles

## PHYLLO

- 1 package (16 ounces) frozen phyllo dough, thawed
- 2 cups butter, melted
- 3 cups filling

Preheat oven to 400 degrees. Lightly butter a baking sheet. Unroll dough and remove 3 sheets. Cover unused dough with plastic wrap to keep sheets from drying out. Brush each sheet lightly with melted butter and stack one on top of the other. Cut stack in half to yield two 9 x 11-inch stacks. Then cut each stack into 5 strips about 2 x 9-inches. Place a rounded teaspoon of filling at end of each strip. Fold over corner diagonally to form a triangle. Continue folding flag-fashion to opposite end. Brush bottoms and tops with butter and place on prepared pan. Repeat process until all dough is used. Bake until light golden brown, 10 to 15 minutes.

*Triangles may be frozen on a baking sheet and then placed in an airtight container. Bake frozen triangles until light golden brown, 15 minutes.*

SERVINGS
60 triangles

## FETA CHEESE FILLING

- 8 ounces feta cheese, crumbled
- 2 cups large-curd cottage cheese
- 1 package (8 ounces) cream cheese, softened
- 3 eggs
- 2 tablespoons minced fresh parsley
- Pinch of white pepper

Combine all ingredients in food processor until smooth. Yields 2½ cups.

SERVINGS
60 triangles

# Crab Filling

Sauté onions and garlic in butter until tender, 5 to 8 minutes. Add remaining ingredients and stir until cream cheese melts. Cool. Yields 3 cups.

**¼ cup sliced green onions**
**1 clove garlic, minced**
**1 tablespoon butter**
**1 pound cooked, shredded crabmeat (or shrimp)**
**1 package (8 ounces) cream cheese, cut into cubes**
**3 tablespoons dry sherry**
**½ tablespoon dried dill weed**
**½ tablespoon Dijon mustard**
**⅛ teaspoon salt**

SERVINGS
60 triangles

# Spinach Filling

Microwave spinach until wilted, 3 minutes. Cool spinach, squeeze dry, then chop. Sauté onion in oil until tender, 5 to 8 minutes. Remove from heat and stir in spinach and remaining ingredients. Yields 1½ cups.

**1 pound fresh spinach, stems removed**
**½ cup diced onion**
**2 tablespoons olive oil**
**½ cup finely chopped pecans, toasted**
**3 tablespoons fresh lemon juice**
**½ teaspoon salt**
**¼ teaspoon black pepper**

SERVINGS
60 triangles

# Artichoke Filling

In a medium bowl combine all ingredients until well blended. Yields 2 cups.

**1 can (14 ounces) artichoke hearts, drained and diced**
**½ cup sour cream**
**1 cup (4 ounces) grated cheddar cheese**
**2 cloves garlic, minced**
**1 teaspoon dried oregano**

SERVINGS
16

# Caramel Brie with Fresh Fruit

Place Brie on a large serving plate. Melt butter in a saucepan. Stir in brown sugar, corn syrup and flour. Bring mixture to a boil, reduce heat and simmer for 5 minutes, stirring constantly. Remove from heat and cool to lukewarm. Gradually stir in milk. Pour mixture over Brie, allowing excess to drip down sides. Sprinkle with toasted pecans. Toss fruit with lemon juice and water just before serving and arrange around Brie.

**1 round (16 ounces) Brie cheese**
**2 tablespoons butter**
**¾ cup packed brown sugar**
**¼ cup light corn syrup**
**1½ tablespoons all-purpose flour**
**¼ cup milk**
**½ cup coarsely chopped pecans, toasted**
**¼ cup water**
**1 tablespoon fresh lemon juice**
**Fresh pears and apples, cut into wedges**

SERVINGS
3-4 cups

# Mushroom Walnut Pâté

Sauté mushrooms, onions and thyme in butter until onions are tender, 5 to 8 minutes. Add sherry and salt and continue cooking until liquid is almost evaporated. Remove from heat and cool. Combine mushroom mixture with cream cheese and blend thoroughly. Stir in walnuts, parsley and hot pepper sauce. Spread in serving dish, cover and chill for 2 hours. Sprinkle chives on top and serve with assorted crackers.

**1 pound fresh mushrooms, diced**
**½ cup sliced green onions, white part only**
**¼ teaspoon dried thyme**
**¼ cup butter**
**⅓ cup dry sherry**
**1 teaspoon salt**
**1 package (8 ounces) cream cheese, softened**
**1 cup finely chopped walnuts, toasted**
**¼ cup minced fresh parsley**
**Dash hot pepper sauce**
**¼ cup snipped fresh chives for garnish**

SERVINGS
6 cups

# PERFECT PÂTÉ

Sauté chicken livers in ¼ cup butter until tender, about 10 minutes. Remove from pan and set aside. Sauté mushrooms and onions in ¼ cup butter until tender, 5 to 8 minutes. Stir in chicken livers, garlic, parsley and wine. Cook over low heat for 20 minutes. While hot, transfer to food processor and purée. Cool completely and stir in 1½ cups butter, mustard, salt and pepper. Spoon into serving dish or ramekins. Cover and chill for 2 hours. Serve at room temperature with crackers or small toast points.

*Pâté freezes well. Thaw overnight in refrigerator.*

2 pounds chicken livers, drained
½ cup butter, divided
¼ pound fresh mushrooms, sliced
1 bunch green onions, thinly sliced
2 cloves garlic, minced
1 bunch fresh parsley, minced
1 cup dry white wine
1½ cups butter, softened
½ cup Dijon mustard
Salt and freshly ground pepper, to taste

**Ask your child what he wants for dinner only if he's buying.**

*Fran Lebowitz*

SERVINGS
24

# FRITTATA BASKETS

Preheat oven to 350 degrees. Lightly grease two 12-count muffin pans. Thaw spinach and squeeze dry. Beat together eggs and egg whites in a large bowl. Add spinach, cheeses, mushrooms, onion and seasonings. Mix well. Cut each tortilla into quarters and place in muffin pans to form cups. Fill each cup with a heaping tablespoon of cheese mixture and bake for 20 minutes.

- 1 package (10 ounces) frozen chopped spinach
- 2 eggs
- 4 egg whites
- 1½ cups freshly grated Parmesan cheese
- 1 cup low-fat ricotta cheese
- 1 cup low-fat cottage cheese
- ¼ cup diced fresh mushrooms
- ¼ cup diced onion
- ½ teaspoon salt
- ½ teaspoon dried oregano
- 6 flour tortillas (8-inch)

SERVINGS
12 mushrooms

# SAUSAGE & FENNEL MUSHROOM CAPS

Preheat oven to 450 degrees. Grease a 13 x 9-inch baking dish. In a small skillet crumble and brown sausage until thoroughly cooked. Remove sausage and drain, reserving 2 tablespoons of drippings. Stir fennel seed into sausage and set aside. Sauté onion and garlic in drippings until tender. Stir in flour and cook for 2 minutes. Remove from heat, stir in sour cream, sausage mixture and parsley. Season to taste and set aside. Remove and discard mushroom stems. Brush each cap with olive oil and fill generously with stuffing mixture. Arrange in prepared dish. Sprinkle tops with cheese and bake uncovered until bubbly, 15 minutes. Cool slightly before serving.

- ⅓ pound Italian sausage, casings removed
- ¼ teaspoon fennel seed
- ¼ cup minced onion
- 1 clove garlic, minced
- 1 tablespoon all-purpose flour
- ⅓ cup sour cream
- ¼ cup minced fresh parsley
- Salt and freshly ground pepper, to taste
- 12 large, fresh white mushrooms
- ¼ cup freshly grated Parmesan cheese
- Olive oil

SERVINGS
40-48 pieces

# CHICKEN SATAY

Cut chicken breasts into 1-inch pieces and set aside. Combine remaining ingredients in a medium bowl and mix well. Add chicken and stir to coat. Cover and chill for 4 to 8 hours. Remove chicken and thread on thin skewers. Grill or broil until cooked, 10 to 15 minutes. Serve hot.

- 1 pound chicken breasts, skinned and boned
- ¼ cup smooth peanut butter
- 2 tablespoons minced onion
- 2 tablespoons fresh lemon juice
- 1½ teaspoons soy sauce
- 1 clove garlic, minced
- ½ teaspoon coriander
- ⅛ teaspoon ground red pepper
- 2 tablespoons minced fresh parsley

SERVINGS
24 pieces

# SEVEN SPICE SHRIMP

Preheat oven to 375 degrees. In a food processor blend parsley, onion, garlic, vinegar, dill, mustard seed, coriander, red pepper, allspice, cloves and salt. Scrape down sides, add oil in a steady stream and blend until smooth. In a baking dish large enough to hold shrimp in a single layer, toss shrimp, spice mixture and bay leaf. Bake uncovered until shrimp are opaque, 15 to 20 minutes. Discard bay leaf and serve with cocktail picks. Serve crusty French bread as an accompaniment to dip in sauce.

- ½ cup fresh parsley leaves, loosely packed
- 1 small onion, coarsely chopped
- 1 clove garlic, peeled
- 2 tablespoons white wine vinegar
- ½ teaspoon dried dill weed
- ½ teaspoon mustard seed
- ½ teaspoon ground coriander
- ¼ teaspoon ground red pepper
- ¼ teaspoon ground allspice
- ⅛ teaspoon ground cloves
- ½ teaspoon salt
- ⅓ cup olive oil
- 1½ pounds large shrimp (about 24), shelled and deveined
- 1 bay leaf
- 1 loaf French bread

SERVINGS
50-60 pieces

# STUFFED GRAPE LEAVES WITH CHICKEN

- 1½ pounds lean coarsely ground beef
- ¾ cup long-grain white rice
- 6 tablespoons water
- 6 tablespoons butter, softened
- ¾ teaspoon ground cinnamon
- ¼ teaspoon ground allspice (optional)
- 1½ teaspoons salt
- ¼ teaspoon black pepper
- 1 quart preserved grape leaves
- 1½ pounds chicken drummettes
- 6 cloves garlic, peeled
- 2 cups boiling water
- ½ cup fresh lemon juice
- 1 cup plain yogurt
- 1 clove garlic, minced
- ½ teaspoon salt
- 1 tablespoon dried mint, crushed

Mix together beef, rice, water, butter, cinnamon, allspice, salt and pepper. Place grape leaf smooth side down on work surface. Cut off stem. Place a heaping teaspoon of beef mixture in an oblong shape at base of leaf. Roll up, tucking in excess leaf at sides to make a tiny bundle. Repeat with remaining filling.

Line bottom of Dutch oven with half the plain leaves. Arrange chicken drummettes on top of leaves. Sprinkle with whole cloves of garlic. Arrange stuffed grape leaves in layers, seam side down, on top of drummettes. Top with remaining plain grape leaves. Invert saucer on top of leaves to weight down. Add boiling water and lemon juice. Bring to a boil, reduce heat, cover and simmer for 1 hour.

Combine yogurt, garlic, salt and mint. Cover and chill for at least 1 hour.

Remove Dutch oven from heat and let stand for 1 hour. Remove saucer, drain liquid and discard top layer of plain leaves. Arrange stuffed grape leaves on serving platter and surround with chicken. Discard garlic and layer of plain leaves. Serve hot or cold with sauce.

SERVINGS
32 pieces

# CURRIED CHICKEN PUFFS

PUFFS:
¼ cup butter
½ cup water
½ cup all-purpose flour
Pinch of salt
2 eggs, room temperature
CURRIED CHICKEN FILLING:
1½ cups sliced almonds
1 tablespoon butter
1 package (8 ounces) cream cheese
¼ cup mayonnaise
2 cups cooked, diced chicken
3 tablespoons chopped chutney
2 teaspoons curry powder
1 teaspoon salt

Preheat oven to 400 degrees. Lightly grease two large baking sheets. In a medium saucepan bring butter and water to a boil. Add flour and salt all at once. Using a wooden spoon, stir vigorously over low heat until mixture leaves sides of pan and forms a ball. Remove from heat. Add eggs one at a time, beating vigorously after each until mixture is smooth and glossy. Drop dough by rounded teaspoons onto prepared sheets, making 32 small puffs. Bake until puffed and firm to the touch, 15 to 20 minutes. Cool completely. Cut off top of each puff and fill with chicken mixture.

Curried Chicken Filling: Sauté almonds in butter until lightly browned. In a large bowl blend cream cheese and mayonnaise. Stir in almonds and remaining ingredients and chill.

*Curried Chicken Filling makes a nice spread for tea sandwiches.*

Cooking is like love.
It should be entered
into with abandon
or not at all.

*Harriet Van Horne*

SERVINGS
20 pieces

# CHILI BACON GRISSINI

Preheat oven to 350 degrees. Wrap one bacon slice in a spiral around each breadstick. Bacon should cover half of breadstick. On a sheet of waxed paper sift together sugar and chili powder. Roll each breadstick in mixture, coating bacon well. Arrange ½ inch apart on broiler pan. Bake until coating is caramelized and bacon is golden brown, 20 minutes. Carefully loosen breadsticks and cool in pan until firm, about 10 minutes. Bacon will become crisp and breadsticks will harden as they cool. Serve at room temperature.

**20 slices bacon, room temperature**
**20 long thin breadsticks (grissini)**
**⅓ cup packed brown sugar**
**3 tablespoons chili powder**

SERVINGS
36-48 pieces

# SUMMER QUESADILLAS

Sauté onion, bell pepper and garlic in oil until tender, 5 to 8 minutes. Add zucchini and cook for 6 minutes. Season with salt and cool. Spread ½ cup zucchini mixture on each of 6 tortillas. Sprinkle each with grated cheese and top with another tortilla. Lightly oil skillet and brown each quesadilla on both sides until golden. Cut into wedges and serve warm with Salsa Fresca (page 32).

**½ cup diced red onion**
**½ red bell pepper, diced**
**2 cloves garlic, minced**
**1 tablespoon vegetable oil**
**2 small zucchini, shredded**
**½ teaspoon salt**
**12 flour tortillas (8-inch)**
**4 cups (16 ounces) grated Monterey Jack cheese with jalapeño peppers**

SERVINGS
100 pieces

# Glazed Meatballs

Combine ketchup, brown sugar, onion, garlic and liquid smoke in a 2-quart saucepan. Bring mixture to a boil, cook for 1 minute and set aside.

Preheat oven to 350 degrees. Mix meatball ingredients in a large bowl. Moisten hands and roll mixture into 1-inch balls. Place meatballs close together in two 13 x 9-inch nonmetallic baking dishes. Pour sauce over top and bake uncovered for 30 minutes.

**SAUCE:**
- 2 cups ketchup
- 2 cups packed brown sugar
- ¼ cup minced onion
- 1 clove garlic, minced
- 2 tablespoons liquid smoke (optional)

**MEATBALLS:**
- 2 pounds lean ground beef
- 1 pound pork sausage
- ½ cup bread crumbs
- 2 eggs, lightly beaten
- 1 cup diced onion
- ½ cup minced parsley
- 2 cloves garlic, minced
- 2 tablespoon Worchestershire sauce

SERVINGS
24 sandwiches

# Party Sandwiches

Preheat oven to 350 degrees. Combine mustard, onion, Worcestershire sauce, butter and poppy seed. Spread mixture on half of each bun and top with roast beef and ½ slice cheese. Wrap sandwiches in foil and heat for 15 to 20 minutes. (May be frozen before baking. Heat for 35 to 40 minutes.)

For variety, use smoked turkey and Monterey Jack cheese, corned beef and Swiss cheese, or shredded ham and baby Swiss cheese. Croissants or potato rolls may also be used for luncheon sandwiches.

*Heat ahead and place in an ice chest. Sandwiches will stay warm for a long time.*

- 3 tablespoons prepared mustard
- ¼ cup minced onion or ¼ cup thinly sliced green onions
- 1 tablespoon Worcestershire sauce
- ¾ cup butter, softened
- 1 teaspoon poppy seed
- 24 cocktail buns, split
- 2 pounds shredded roast beef
- 12 slices Havarti cheese

SERVINGS
100 pieces

# Black Bean Spinners

Mash beans to desired consistency. Stir in onions, garlic powder, cumin and red pepper. Cook over medium heat, stirring frequently until thoroughly heated. Soften tortillas in microwave for 10 seconds. Spread mixture in a thin layer on tortillas and roll up. Cut into ¾-inch slices, discarding ends. Serve at room temperature with Salsa Classico.

- 3 cans (15 ounces each) black beans, with liquid
- 1 cup thinly sliced green onions
- 1 teaspoon garlic powder
- 1 teaspoon ground cumin
- ¼ teaspoon ground red pepper
- 10 flour tortillas (10-inch)

SERVINGS
100 pieces

# Chicken Spinners

Beat cream cheese in a medium bowl until smooth. Stir in chicken, cheese, onions, olives and green chilies and mix well. Spread mixture in a thin layer on tortillas and roll up. Cover tightly with plastic wrap and chill for at least 2 hours. Cut into ¾-inch slices, discarding ends. Serve with guacamole, sour cream and Salsa Classico.

- 2 packages (8 ounces each) cream cheese, softened
- 2½ cups cooked, diced chicken breast
- 1½ cups (6 ounces) grated sharp cheddar cheese
- 1 bunch green onions, thinly sliced
- 1 jar (4 ounces) stuffed green olives, drained and diced
- 1 can (4¼ ounces) chopped black olives
- 1 can (4½ ounces) chopped green chilies
- 10 flour tortillas (10-inch)

SERVINGS
100 pieces

# Beef Spinners

In a large bowl beat cream cheese, picante sauce, garlic powder and Worcestershire sauce until smooth. Stir in beef and onion tops. If mixture is too thick add milk, 1 teaspoon at a time, until thin enough to spread. Divide mixture among tortillas and spread to within ½ inch of edge. Roll up tortillas tightly. Chill for 1 to 2 hours. Cut into ¾-inch slices, discarding ends, and serve with Salsa Classico.

- 2 packages (8 ounces each) cream cheese, softened
- 2 tablespoons picante sauce
- 1 teaspoon garlic powder
- Dash Worcestershire sauce
- 1 package (2½ ounces) dried beef, chopped
- 1 bunch green onion tops, sliced
- Milk
- 10 flour tortillas (10-inch)

SERVINGS
4 cups

# Salsa Classico

Purée all ingredients in food processor until smooth. Serve with Spinners or tortilla chips.

- 2 cans (15 ounces each) stewed tomatoes, drained
- 1 can (4½ ounces) chopped green chilies
- 4 serrano peppers, seeded and chopped
- ½ white onion, coarsely chopped
- 2 tablespoons fresh lime juice
- ¼ cup minced fresh cilantro
- 1 teaspoon ground cumin
- 1 teaspoon salt
- 1 teaspoon granulated sugar

SERVINGS
48 pieces

# LAVOSH TOSTADA

Preheat oven to 350 degrees. Combine cheeses, olives, green chilies and jalapeño peppers. Place each lavosh cracker on a baking sheet. Spread half of mixture to edge of one cracker. Repeat with remaining mixture on second cracker. Bake until cheese has melted, 15 minutes. Cut in pieces and serve warm.

- 4 cups (16 ounces) grated sharp cheddar cheese
- 4 cups (16 ounces) grated mozzarella cheese
- 2 cans (2¼ ounces each) sliced black olives, drained
- 1 can (4½ ounces) chopped green chilies
- 1 cup jalapeño pepper slices, drained
- 2 large lavosh crackers

SERVINGS
1½ cups

# A MAJOR SPREAD

Cook bacon until crisp. Drain, crumble and set aside. In a small bowl mix cream cheese, chutney, curry powder and mustard until creamy. Stir in bacon. Chill for several hours and serve garnished with peanuts and paprika.

*Chilled mixture may be formed into one or two cheese balls rolled in peanuts and paprika or used as a spread for tea sandwiches.*

- 4 slices bacon
- 1 package (8 ounces) cream cheese, softened
- ½ cup Major Grey's chutney, chopped
- 1 teaspoon curry powder
- ¼ teaspoon dry mustard
- ¼ cup dry roasted peanuts, chopped
- Paprika

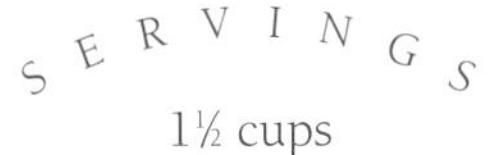


1½ cups

# THAI SAUCE

Combine all ingredients and blend well. Serve with sliced apples and crackers.

⅔ cup crunchy peanut butter
⅓ cup packed brown sugar
¼ cup chili sauce
2 tablespoons fresh lemon juice
1 teaspoon soy sauce
¼ to ½ teaspoon crushed red pepper

One cannot
think well,
love well,
sleep well,
if one has not
dined well.

*Virginia Woolf*

SERVINGS
4 cups

# Salsa Fresca

Combine all ingredients, cover and chill for 2 hours. Serve with Lean Tortilla Chips.

- 4 large or 5 medium tomatoes, seeded and diced
- 1 can (4½ ounces) chopped green chilies
- 1 can (4¼ ounces) chopped black olives
- 1 bunch green onions, thinly sliced
- 3 tablespoons vegetable oil
- 1 tablespoon vinegar
- 1 clove garlic, minced
- Pinch of dried oregano
- Pinch of dried basil
- 1 teaspoon salt
- ¼ teaspoon black pepper

SERVINGS
6 cups

# Salsa del Mar

Combine avocados, shrimp, onions, tomatoes, cilantro, salt and pepper. In small bowl whisk oil, vinegar, cumin, red pepper and garlic until well blended. Stir into avocado mixture. Cover and chill for 1 hour.

- 5 ripe avocados, diced
- 1 pound tiny shrimp, cooked
- 5 green onions, sliced
- 5 tomatoes, seeded and diced
- 1 bunch fresh cilantro, minced
- Salt and freshly ground pepper, to taste
- 6 tablespoons olive oil
- 2 tablespoons red wine vinegar
- 2 teaspoons ground cumin
- ½ teaspoon ground red pepper
- 4 cloves garlic, minced

SERVINGS
80 chips

# LEAN TORTILLA CHIPS

10 flour or corn tortillas
(8 or 10-inch)

Preheat oven to 350 degrees. Cut tortillas into eighths. Arrange on baking sheet without overlapping. Toast in oven until lightly browned, about 8 minutes for flour tortillas and 10 minutes for corn tortillas.

*A tasty low-fat alternative to commercial chips!*

SERVINGS
80 chips

# FAT TORTILLA CHIPS

10 flour or corn tortillas
(8 or 10-inch)
Vegetable oil
Sea Salt

Cut tortillas into eighths. Fry in hot oil until crispy, 5 to 10 seconds per side. Drain on paper towels and sprinkle with salt. Serve immediately.

*Worth the calories!*

Too much of a
good thing can
be wonderful.

*Mae West*

SERVINGS
4 cups

# Spicy Artichoke Dip

Preheat oven to 325 degrees. Purée all ingredients in food processor until smooth. Spread mixture in a shallow 9-inch baking dish. Bake uncovered until lightly browned on top, 30 to 45 minutes. Serve with lavosh crackers or tortilla chips.

- 1 can (14 ounces) artichoke hearts, drained
- 1 cup freshly grated Parmesan cheese
- ½ cup sour cream
- ½ cup mayonnaise
- 1 package (8 ounces) cream cheese
- 2 cloves garlic, minced
- 2 jalapeño peppers, seeded and diced
- ½ teaspoon salt

SERVINGS
2½ cups

# Fresh Cucumber Dip

Beat cream cheese until smooth. Add mayonnaise and lemon juice and continue beating until blended. Stir in cucumbers, onions, dill, hot pepper sauce and salt until well mixed. Cover and chill for at least 3 hours. Serve with assorted crudités and crackers.

- 1 package (8 ounces) cream cheese, softened
- ½ cup mayonnaise
- 1 tablespoon fresh lemon juice
- 2 medium cucumbers peeled, seeded and diced
- 4 green onions, thinly sliced
- 2 teaspoons snipped fresh dill
- ¾ teaspoon hot pepper sauce
- ¼ teaspoon salt

SERVINGS
3½ cups

# PRETZEL PEPPER DIP

Beat cream cheese, butter, dip mix and Parmesan cheese until smooth. Spread in shallow serving dish and cover generously with pepper. Serve with pretzel knots and chips.

- 3 packages (8 ounces each) cream cheese, softened
- ½ cup butter, softened
- 1 package (1 ounce) ranch-style dip mix
- ¼ cup grated Parmesan cheese
- Cracked pepper
- Pretzel knots
- Pretzel chips

Age is something that doesn't matter, unless you are a cheese.

*Billie Burke*

SERVINGS
3 tablespoons dry mix
enough for 9 recipes

# Boursin Mix

Combine all ingredients. Store in an airtight container. When ready to serve, combine 1 teaspoon of mix with 1 package (3 ounces) softened cream cheese and 1 tablespoon softened butter. Serve with crackers or crudités. May also be used as a filling for snow peas.

**1 teaspoon garlic powder**
**2 teaspoons dried oregano**
**1 teaspoon dried dill weed**
**1 teaspoon dried marjoram**
**1 teaspoon dried basil**
**1 teaspoon dried thyme**
**2 teaspoons freshly ground pepper**

SERVINGS
1⅓ cups dry mix
enough for 4 recipes

# Dill Dip Mix

Combine all ingredients. Store in an airtight container. When ready to serve, combine ⅓ cup of mix with 1 cup sour cream and ½ cup mayonnaise. Cover and chill for at least 2 hours to allow flavors to blend. Serve with crudités.

*Dry mixes make nice gifts.*

**½ cup dried parsley flakes**
**½ cup dried minced onion**
**3 tablespoons Beau Monde seasoning**
**3 tablespoons dried dill weed**

SERVINGS
16 cups

# DooDah Doodles

1 box (10 ounces) miniature round butter crackers
1 box (10 ounces) thin wheat crackers
1 box (10 ounces) mini pretzel knots
1 can (12 ounces) mixed nuts
1 package (1 ounce) ranch-style dressing mix
1 teaspoon dried dill weed
1 teaspoon garlic salt
⅔ cup vegetable oil

Preheat oven to 200 degrees. Combine crackers, pretzels, nuts, dressing mix, dill weed and garlic salt in a large roasting pan. Pour oil over dry mixture and stir gently to combine. Bake for 20 minutes, stirring occasionally. Store in an airtight container.

No problem is too big to handle
if we just stop and look deep
within that special place . . .
the refrigerator.

*Cathy Guisewite*

SERVINGS
4 cups

# PEPPERED PECANS

Preheat oven to 275 degrees. Spread pecans evenly in a jelly-roll pan and drizzle with butter. Bake until lightly browned, 20 to 25 minutes. In a large bowl mix soy sauce, salt and hot pepper sauce. Add pecans and toss. Let stand for at least 30 minutes then drain on paper towels. Store in an airtight container.

**1 pound (4 cups) pecan halves**
**½ cup butter, melted**
**2 tablespoons soy sauce**
**1 teaspoon salt**
**¼ teaspoon hot pepper sauce**

SERVINGS
1½ cups

# BREW NUTS

Melt butter in heavy skillet over medium heat. Add brown sugar and curry powder, stirring until sugar is dissolved. Add peanuts and cook for 3 to 4 minutes, stirring constantly. Remove from skillet. Cool on foil, separating nuts. Store in an airtight container.

**1 tablespoon butter**
**3 tablespoons packed brown sugar**
**1 teaspoon curry powder**
**1½ cups dry roasted peanuts**

SERVINGS 24

# Carry's Cranberry Wassail

Combine honey, water, cloves and cinnamon in a small saucepan. Bring to a boil, reduce heat and simmer for 20 minutes. Remove cloves and cinnamon sticks. In a 5-quart pan combine juices and honey mixture. Simmer for 1 hour. Add cranberries and serve hot.

**½ cup honey**
**½ cup water**
**12 whole cloves**
**2 cinnamon sticks**
**48 ounces cranberry juice**
**3 cups orange juice**
**32 ounces apple cider**
**Fresh cranberries for garnish**

SERVINGS 10

# Orange Blush

Combine orange juice, cranberry juice and sugar and stir until sugar is dissolved. Chill. Just before serving, stir in club soda and pour over crushed ice.

**1 can (12 ounces) frozen orange juice, thawed**
**2 cups cranberry juice**
**½ cup granulated sugar**
**32 ounces club soda or champagne, chilled**

SERVINGS
4

# APRICOT BANANA FRAPPÉ

Blend ingredients in food processor on high for 1 minute. Pour into goblets and garnish.

**2 cups apricot nectar**
**½ cup fresh orange juice**
**2 tablespoons fresh lemon juice**
**½ cup plain yogurt**
**2 ripe bananas, sliced**
**1 cup crushed ice**
**Mint leaves or orange slices for garnish**

SERVINGS
10

# SUNSET SANGRIA

Combine orange juice and sugar in a saucepan. Bring mixture to a boil over medium heat, stirring occasionally until sugar is dissolved. Reduce heat and simmer for 5 minutes. Cool for 20 minutes. Add orange and lime slices and chill for at least 4 hours. Fill a large pitcher one-third full with crushed ice and add fruit mixture, mashing fruit slightly to release flavor. Add wine and stir.

**1½ cups fresh orange juice**
**1 cup granulated sugar**
**1 large orange, thinly sliced**
**1 lime, thinly sliced**
**Crushed ice**
**2 bottles (750 milliliters each)**
**Burgundy wine**

SERVINGS
10

# SANGRIA BLANCA

Combine all ingredients except club soda in a large glass pitcher and chill. Just before serving, fill large wine glasses half full, spooning several pieces of fruit into each. Add ice and fill with club soda.

1 bottle (750 milliliters)
  dry white wine
Juice of 1 orange
1 orange, thinly sliced
1 lime, thinly sliced
1 lemon, thinly sliced
1 peach, peeled and sliced
¼ cup superfine sugar
32 ounces club soda, chilled

Wine is earth's
answer to the sun.

*Margaret Fuller*

SERVINGS 16

# Prohibition Punch

Mix lemonade, pineapple juice and water. Pour into punch bowl. Slowly add ginger ale and sparkling grape juice. Stir gently until mixed.

*Even Ms. Nation would approve!*

- 1 can (6 ounces) frozen lemonade, thawed
- 1 can (6 ounces) frozen pineapple juice, thawed
- 3 cups cold water
- 28 ounces ginger ale, chilled
- 25 ounces sparkling white Catawba grape juice or nonalcoholic champagne, chilled

SERVINGS 4

# Coffee Alexander

Whip 1 cup cream until it starts to thicken. Add sugar and beat until thick enough to hold firm peaks. Cover and chill.

In a 4-cup glass measure, combine coffee, brandy, ½ cup cream and crème de cacao. Microwave on high for 3 minutes. Pour into coffee mugs. Garnish each serving with whipped cream and shaved chocolate.

- 1½ cups heavy cream, divided
- 2 tablespoons confectioners' sugar
- 2 cups strongly brewed coffee
- ¼ cup brandy
- 2 tablespoons crème de cacao
- Shaved chocolate or chocolate curls for garnish

SERVINGS 24

# GOLDEN PUNCH

Chill champagne, Sauterne and club soda. Place ice cubes in punch bowl. Mix brandy, Cointreau and corn syrup and pour over ice. Stir in champagne, Sauterne and club soda. Stir in strawberries and mint sprigs.

2 fifths champagne
1 fifth Sauterne
32 ounces club soda
4 to 6 cups ice cubes
¼ cup brandy
¼ cup Cointreau liqueur
¼ cup light corn syrup
1 cup sliced fresh strawberries
Mint sprigs for garnish

The next best thing to being clever is being able to quote someone who is.

*Mary Pettibone Poole*

# MOVIN' AND SHAKIN'

## How a woman in her salad days ended up in hot soup.

It was that time in America when salad was for rabbits and soup was for tricking the family into eating leftovers. ❖ Then she came sizzling out of the humid, tropical broth of Rio de Janeiro, shaking her spicy Brazilian cruet to the delight of salad lovers everywhere. ❖ ***Ayy, carrumba!*** ❖ Just two rhumbas and half a samba later, Carmen Miranda merenquéd onto the shores of a meat-and-potatoes North America that was just waiting for a taste of something hot and spicy. ❖ Needless to say, we embraced her like a mug of hot chili on a winter afternoon. We loved the costume, especially that hat. It was a fruit salad waiting to happen. What red-blooded American didn't want to peel that hat, dice it into a bowl, douse the whole thing in poppy seed dressing and dig in? ❖ Speaking of dressing, it was a lack thereof that eventually landed her in hot soup. ❖ But, that's been forgotten now. All we remember is the salad days of Carmen Miranda, when mothers from Bangor to Barstow admonished their children, "I Yi-Yi-Yi-Yi Like You To Finish Your Waldorf!"

# Soups & Salads

SERVINGS
6

# Sweet Pepper Bisque

In a 3-quart saucepan sauté onion and garlic in butter until tender, 5 to 8 minutes. Add bell pepper and sauté for 5 minutes, then add hot pepper sauce. Stir in flour and cook over low heat for 2 minutes. Whisk in chicken broth and cook over medium heat until mixture thickens slightly. Purée in a food processor until smooth. Return to pan and whisk in half-and-half. Heat to serving temperature and stir in cheese.

1 cup diced onion
1 clove garlic, minced
2 tablespoons butter
2 cups diced red bell pepper
Dash hot pepper sauce
3 tablespoons all-purpose flour
2 cups chicken broth
2 cups half-and-half
1 cup (4 ounces) grated
  Swiss cheese

SERVINGS
8

# Autumn Pumpkin Soup

Sauté onion and leeks in butter in a large saucepan until tender, 5 to 8 minutes. Stir in chicken broth and pumpkin and heat thoroughly. Add salt and white pepper. Purée in food processor until smooth. Add sugar, nutmeg, lemon juice and orange zest. Return to pan and slowly whisk in half-and-half. Heat to serving temperature. Sprinkle with sunflower kernels.

1 cup diced onion
2 tablespoons diced leeks,
  white part only
1 tablespoon butter
3 cups chicken broth
1 can (16 ounces) solid
  pack pumpkin
½ teaspoon salt
Freshly ground white pepper,
  to taste
½ teaspoon granulated sugar
¼ teaspoon ground nutmeg
1 tablespoon fresh lemon juice
1 tablespoon grated orange zest
½ cup half-and-half
⅓ cup roasted sunflower kernels

SERVINGS 8

# WILD MUSHROOM BISQUE

Remove stems from 6 mushrooms. Slice caps and set aside. Chop stems and remaining mushrooms. In a 3-quart saucepan simmer chicken broth, chopped mushrooms and onion for 30 minutes. Purée in food processor until smooth. Melt 7 tablespoons butter in a large saucepan and stir in flour until well blended. Add milk and continue stirring until sauce thickens. Stir in cream, mushroom purée and seasonings. Just before serving, sauté reserved mushroom slices in 1 tablespoon butter. Heat soup to serving temperature, stir in sherry and garnish with mushroom slices.

1 pound assorted fresh mushrooms (shiitake, portobello, porcini, morels)
4 cups chicken broth
1 medium onion, diced
½ cup butter, divided
½ cup all-purpose flour
3 cups hot milk
1 cup heavy cream
1 teaspoon salt
White pepper, to taste
Hot pepper sauce, to taste
2 tablespoons dry sherry

I've been on a diet for two weeks and all I've lost is two weeks.

*Totie Fields*

SERVINGS
10-12

# Chive & Cheese Soup

Sauté leeks in butter with celery in a 4-quart stock pot until leeks are tender, about 8 minutes. Stir in flour and cook for 3 minutes. Add chicken broth, water and salt. Bring to a boil, stirring occasionally. Reduce heat and simmer partially covered for 15 minutes. In a medium bowl beat cream cheese, yogurt and egg yolks until smooth. Gradually add 2 cups soup mixture and blend. Stir back into soup and heat to serving temperature. Do not boil. Season with white pepper and sprinkle with chives.

6 leeks, diced, white part only
6 tablespoons butter
4 stalks celery, diced
6 tablespoons all-purpose flour
5 cups chicken broth
3 cups water
1 teaspoon salt
2 packages (8 ounces each) cream cheese, softened
1½ to 2 cups plain yogurt, room temperature
4 egg yolks, beaten
Freshly ground white pepper, to taste
¼ cup snipped fresh chives

SERVINGS
6

# Crab & Asparagus Soup

Cover mushrooms with warm water and soak for 30 minutes. Drain, reserving water. Cut away tough stems and slice caps into ¼-inch strips. In a 4-quart saucepan combine reserved mushroom water, chicken broth and onions. Bring to a boil, reduce heat and simmer until onions are tender, 5 minutes. Stir in crabmeat, asparagus and mushroom strips. Bring to a boil, then reduce heat. Stir cornstarch into cold water and add to soup. Simmer, stirring constantly, until soup thickens and clears. Serve with green onions sprinkled on top.

5 dried Chinese mushrooms
1 cup warm water
6 cups chicken broth
1 small onion, cut lengthwise into ¼-inch strips
1 pound fresh or canned crabmeat
1 pound fresh asparagus spears, cut diagonally into 1½-inch pieces
1 teaspoon cornstarch
½ cup cold water
2 green onions, thinly sliced

SERVINGS 6

# Spinach Watercress Potage

Trim 1 inch from stems of watercress. Simmer chicken broth, watercress, spinach and onion in a large saucepan for 15 minutes. Purée in food processor until smooth. Blend in flour and butter. Return to pan and slowly whisk in cream, nutmeg, salt and pepper. Simmer until thoroughly heated, 6 to 8 minutes. Soup may be served hot or cold.

- 1 bunch fresh watercress
- 2 cups chicken broth
- 1 package (10 ounces) frozen spinach, partially thawed
- 1 small onion, diced
- 3 tablespoons all-purpose flour
- 3 tablespoons butter
- ½ cup heavy cream
- ¼ teaspoon ground nutmeg
- Salt and freshly ground pepper, to taste

SERVINGS 6

# Vegetable Lentil Soup

In a 5-quart Dutch oven over medium heat, sauté carrots, celery, onion and garlic in oil until tender, 5 to 8 minutes. Stir in tomatoes, lentils, chicken broth, potatoes and water. Stir with spoon to break up tomatoes. Add salt and pepper. Bring to a boil, reduce heat, cover and simmer for 1 hour. Just before serving, stir spinach into soup. Simmer until spinach wilts, 10 minutes.

- 2 medium carrots, sliced
- 2 medium stalks celery, sliced
- 1 medium onion, diced
- 1 clove garlic, minced
- 2 tablespoons olive oil
- 1 can (14 ounces) Italian-style stewed tomatoes
- 1 cup dry lentils
- 2 cans (14½ ounces each) chicken broth
- ¾ pound red potatoes, diced
- 3 cups water
- Salt and freshly ground pepper, to taste
- ½ pound fresh spinach, stems removed and thinly sliced

SERVINGS
6

# WILD RICE & CHICKEN SOUP

Combine chicken broth, wild rice, celery, onion and carrot in a 3-quart saucepan. Bring to a boil, reduce heat and simmer covered until rice is tender, about 45 minutes. Melt butter in a saucepan and stir in flour, salt and pepper. Add milk and whisk over medium heat until thick. Stir into rice mixture then add chicken, almonds and lemon pepper. Simmer until soup is thoroughly heated. Just before serving, stir in sherry.

- 5 cups chicken broth
- ½ cup wild rice
- ½ cup diced celery
- ½ cup diced onion
- ½ cup diced carrot
- 3 tablespoons butter
- 3 tablespoons all-purpose flour
- ½ teaspoon salt
- Freshly ground pepper, to taste
- 1 cup hot milk
- 2 cups cooked, diced chicken
- ¼ cup sliced almonds, toasted
- ¼ teaspoon lemon pepper
- ¼ cup dry sherry

SERVINGS
8-10

# BAKED POTATO SOUP

Cook bacon until crisp. Drain, reserving drippings, crumble and set aside. Pour reserved drippings into a Dutch oven, add butter and melt over medium heat. Sauté onions until tender, 5 to 8 minutes. In a small bowl combine flour and enough chicken broth to make a paste. Stir paste and remaining chicken broth into onions and cook until thickened. Add potatoes, half-and-half, milk, salt and pepper. Heat to serving temperature. Garnish with sour cream, cheese, green onions and bacon.

- 5 slices bacon
- ½ cup butter
- 2 small onions, diced
- ½ cup all-purpose flour
- 3 cups chicken broth
- 4 medium potatoes, baked, peeled and diced
- 1 cup half-and-half
- 2 cups milk
- 2 teaspoons salt
- 1 teaspoon black pepper
- 1 cup sour cream
- 1½ cups (6 ounces) grated cheddar cheese
- 4 green onions, thinly sliced

SERVINGS
18

# POSOLE

Brown chorizo, pork and onions in a large stock pot. Drain well. Add water, garlic, cumin seed, oregano, thyme, bay leaves and salt. Bring to a boil, reduce heat and simmer covered for 2 hours. Remove bay leaves and discard. Add picante sauce, hominy, corn, green chilies and tomatillos. Add more water if necessary and cook for 1 hour. Garnish with grated cheese and crushed tortilla chips.

2 pounds chorizo sausage, casings removed
3 to 4 pounds pork loin, cubed
2 onions, diced
12 cups water
5 cloves garlic, minced
1 tablespoon cumin seed
2 teaspoons dried oregano
1 teaspoon ground thyme
4 bay leaves
1 tablespoon salt
3 cups picante sauce
2 cans (14½ ounces each) hominy, drained
2 cans (14½ ounces each) corn, drained
2 cans (7 ounces each) chopped green chilies
2 cups diced tomatillos or 1 can (14½ ounces) diced tomatoes
2 cups (8 ounces) grated cheddar cheese
Tortilla chips, crushed, for garnish

**You have got to throw feeling into cooking.**

*Rosa Lewis*

SERVINGS
6

# Sausage Corn Chowder

Brown sausage in a Dutch oven. Remove from pan and reserve 1 tablespoon drippings. Sauté onion and bell pepper in reserved drippings until tender. Add chicken broth and potatoes. Bring to a boil, reduce heat and simmer until potatoes are tender, 20 minutes. Stir in corn. Whisk flour into milk and stir into soup. Stir in parsley and turmeric and season to taste. Simmer for 30 minutes.

- 1 pound link sausage, cut into bite-size pieces
- 1 cup diced onion
- ½ cup diced green bell pepper
- 1 can (14½ ounces) chicken broth
- 2 medium potatoes, peeled and diced
- 1 can (15 ounces) cream-style corn
- 2 tablespoons all-purpose flour
- 2 cups milk
- 1 tablespoon minced fresh parsley
- ½ teaspoon ground turmeric
- Salt and freshly ground pepper, to taste

SERVINGS
12

# Country Cabbage Soup

Brown meat in large stockpot with celery, onion and bell pepper. Drain well. Add remaining ingredients and simmer until cabbage is tender, about 45 minutes.

- 2 pounds lean ground round
- 2 stalks celery, thinly sliced
- ½ cup diced onion
- ½ cup diced green bell pepper
- 2 cans (16 ounces each) pinto beans, with liquid
- 2 cans (15 ounces each) chili beans, with liquid
- 2 cans (14½ ounces each) diced tomatoes
- 1 medium head cabbage, coarsely chopped
- 3 teaspoons salt
- 1 teaspoon black pepper

SERVINGS
12

# Chili Blanco

Cut chicken into small pieces and season with white pepper and garlic powder. Sauté chicken in oil in a stockpot for 3 minutes. Add remaining soup ingredients and bring to a boil. Reduce heat and simmer for 30 minutes.

To serve, cut tortillas into ¼-inch strips. Place tortilla strips in individual serving bowls with strips extended beyond edges. Ladle chili into bowls. Garnish with sour cream, cheese and cilantro.

3 pounds chicken thighs, skinned and boned
1½ teaspoons white pepper
1 teaspoon garlic powder
3 tablespoons vegetable oil
1 small onion, diced

2 cans (15 ounces each) Great Northern beans
2 cans (14½ ounces each) chicken broth
2 cans (4½ ounces each) chopped green chilies
1 can (10¾ ounces) cream of chicken soup
3 tablespoons jalapeño pepper juice
2 tablespoons minced fresh cilantro
1 teaspoon salt

GARNISH:

6 to 8 flour tortillas (6-inch)
1 cup sour cream
1½ cups (6 ounces) grated mozzarella cheese
½ cup minced fresh cilantro

SERVINGS
10

# Curried Chicken Soup

Sauté rice, onion and carrot in butter for 5 minutes. Add chicken broth, chicken and curry powder. Cover and simmer until rice is cooked, about 20 minutes. Blend flour into milk and gradually stir into soup until mixture thickens. Just before serving, stir in half-and-half and peas. Heat to serving temperature.

¾ cup long-grain white rice
1 cup diced onion
1 cup diced carrot
½ cup butter
8 cups chicken broth
4 to 6 chicken breast halves, cooked and diced
2 teaspoons curry powder
½ cup all-purpose flour
1 cup milk
1 cup half-and-half
1 cup frozen peas, thawed

SERVINGS
10

# Chicken Tortellini Soup

Combine water, chicken broth, soup, chicken, onion, carrot, vermouth, garlic, basil and oregano in a large stockpot. Bring to a boil, reduce heat and simmer uncovered for 30 to 45 minutes. Add broccoli and tortellini. Simmer until broccoli is tender, 10 minutes. Sprinkle with cheese.

6 cups water
3 cans (14½ ounces each) chicken broth
1 can (10¾ ounces) cream of chicken soup
2 cups cooked, diced chicken breasts
1 cup diced onion
1 cup sliced carrot
½ cup dry vermouth
2 cloves garlic, minced
½ teaspoon dried basil
½ teaspoon dried oregano
1 package (10 ounces) frozen chopped broccoli, thawed
1 package (9 ounces) cheese tortellini, fresh or frozen
¾ cup freshly grated Parmesan cheese

SERVINGS

12

# SOMBRERO SOUP

Brown ground beef and onion in a Dutch oven and drain well. Add chilies, seasoning mix, tomato sauce, tomatoes and beef broth. Bring to a boil, reduce heat and simmer uncovered for 20 minutes. (Soup may be chilled or frozen at this point.) At least 15 minutes before serving, add corn and beans and heat to serving temperature. Garnish with sour cream, grated cheese and corn chips.

2 pounds ground beef
¼ cup diced onion
1 can (4½ ounces) chopped green chilies
2 packages (1 ounce each) taco seasoning mix
2 cans (8 ounces each) tomato sauce
2 cans (14½ ounces each) diced tomatoes
1 can (14½ ounces) beef broth
1 package (10 ounces) frozen corn (optional)
1 can (16 ounces) Mexican-style beans or red kidney beans, drained
1 cup sour cream
1½ cups (6 ounces) grated cheddar cheese
Corn chips for garnish

**Food is the most primitive form of comfort.**

*Sheilah Graham*

SERVINGS
4-6

# Chilled Cucumber Soup

Purée onion, chicken broth, lemon juice, salt, dill and garlic in a food processor. Add sour cream and yogurt and blend for 15 to 20 seconds. Stir in cucumbers. Serve chilled, garnished with dill.

¼ medium onion
1 cup chicken broth
1 tablespoon fresh lemon juice
1 teaspoon salt
1 tablespoon snipped fresh dill
Pinch of garlic powder
1 cup sour cream
1 cup plain yogurt
2 cucumbers, peeled, seeded and diced
Fresh dill for garnish

SERVINGS
8-10

# Gazpacho

Combine all vegetables except avocado in a food processor. Pulse until minced, being careful not to over process. Whisk vinegar, oil, salt, pepper and tomato juice until well blended. Stir into vegetables. Cover and chill for at least 4 hours. Serve chilled, garnished with avocado.

6 large ripe tomatoes, seeded and chopped
2 red bell peppers, coarsely chopped
2 medium yellow onions, coarsely chopped
2 large shallots, coarsely chopped
2 large cucumbers, seeded and coarsely chopped
½ cup red wine vinegar
½ cup olive oil
Salt and freshly ground pepper, to taste
1½ cups tomato juice
1 ripe avocado, diced

SERVINGS
8

# AVGOLEMONO

Combine chicken broth, rice and salt in a large saucepan. Bring to a boil, reduce heat, cover and simmer until rice is tender, about 20 minutes. Remove from heat. Beat eggs until pale yellow, then beat in lemon juice. Slowly stir two cups hot chicken broth into egg mixture and whisk together. Pour egg mixture back into soup. Cook until slightly thickened, stirring constantly. Cool to room temperature, then chill for at least 4 hours. Soup will thicken and settle. Just before serving, stir soup and garnish with lemon slices.

**6 cups chicken broth**
**¼ cup long-grain white rice**
**1 teaspoon salt**
**3 eggs**
**¼ cup fresh lemon juice**
**1 lemon, thinly sliced**

What I love about cooking is that after a hard day, there is something comforting about the fact that if you melt butter and add flour then hot stock, *it will get thick!*

*Nora Ephron*

SERVINGS
12

# SALAD GREENS WITH WARM BRIE DRESSING

Arrange salad greens on plates. Top with pears and walnuts. Spoon Warm Brie Dressing over salad and serve immediately.

Warm Brie Dressing: Heat oils in medium saucepan, add cheese and whisk until melted. Slowly whisk in vinegar, cream, salt and pepper. Cook, stirring constantly until heated, about 10 minutes.

**16 cups assorted salad greens (red leaf, Bibb, green leaf, watercress)**
**3 Bosc pears, thinly sliced**
**¾ cup chopped walnuts, toasted**
**WARM BRIE DRESSING:**
**2 tablespoons walnut oil**
**1 tablespoon vegetable oil**
**8 ounces Brie cheese, rind removed and cut into 1-inch cubes**
**2 tablespoons sherry vinegar**
**½ cup heavy cream**
**¼ teaspoon salt**
**¼ teaspoon black pepper**

SERVINGS
8

# FATTOUCH

Preheat oven to 250 degrees. Split pita bread and bake in oven until crisp, 8 to 10 minutes. Break into 1-inch pieces. In a salad bowl combine lettuce, pita, cucumber, tomatoes, onions, mint and sumac. Whisk dressing ingredients until well blended. Pour dressing over salad and toss.

*Ground sumac seasoning is available in specialty food stores.*

**2 rounds pita bread**
**½ head romaine lettuce, torn**
**½ head iceberg lettuce, torn**
**1 cucumber, peeled and diced**
**4 large tomatoes, diced**
**1 bunch green onions, sliced**
**¼ cup minced fresh mint**
**2 tablespoons ground sumac seasoning**
**DRESSING:**
**¼ cup fresh lemon juice**
**½ cup vegetable oil**
**1 clove garlic, minced**
**1 teaspoon salt**
**1 teaspoon black pepper**

SERVINGS
6

# FIELD GREENS WITH GOAT CHEESE & WALNUTS

Preheat oven to 400 degrees. Roll goat cheese in chopped nuts until well coated. Place cheese in a small baking dish and warm on center rack until soft and walnuts begin to turn golden, about 5 minutes. Toss greens and basil with dressing until well coated. Divide evenly among six plates, mounding in center. Slice each log into six pieces and place two pieces on top of each salad.

Dressing: Whisk vinegar, mustard and oil in a small bowl until well blended. Stir in shallot and orange zest and season to taste.

*A handful of tiny edible flower blossoms (pea, bean or pansy) may be added for color.*

**2 logs (4 ounces each) goat cheese**
**½ cup coarsely chopped walnuts**
**12 cups assorted salad greens**
**½ cup fresh basil leaves, sliced**
**DRESSING:**
**2 tablespoons red wine vinegar**
**½ teaspoon Dijon mustard**
**5 tablespoons extra virgin olive oil**
**1 tablespoon minced shallot**
**Grated zest of ½ orange**
**Salt and freshly ground pepper, to taste**

It's the best thing
I've ever eaten
in the whole world–
this week.

SERVINGS
6

# MIXED GREENS WITH SHERRY VINAIGRETTE

Toss lettuce and watercress together. Pour Sherry Vinaigrette over salad and toss. Garnish with fresh berries and walnuts.

Sherry Vinaigrette: Combine all ingredients in food processor until smooth.

- 1 small head red leaf lettuce, torn
- 1 head Bibb lettuce, torn
- 1 bunch fresh watercress, tough stems removed
- 1 cup fresh blueberries or raspberries, for garnish
- 1 cup walnut halves, toasted

SHERRY VINAIGRETTE:

- 1 shallot or clove garlic, minced
- 1 teaspoon dry mustard
- ½ teaspoon salt
- ¼ teaspoon white pepper
- ¼ cup sherry wine vinegar
- ¼ cup walnut oil
- ½ cup safflower oil

SERVINGS
6-8

# SUNFLOWER SPINACH SALAD

In a salad bowl combine spinach, orange slices, onion and sunflower kernels. Just before serving, add avocado to salad and toss with desired amount of dressing.

Poppy Seed Dressing: Blend vinegar, sugar, lemon juice, dry mustard and salt in a food processor. While processor is running, slowly add oil until well blended. Stir in poppy seed.

- 10 ounces fresh spinach, torn
- 3 medium oranges, peeled and sliced
- ½ small red onion, thinly sliced
- ¼ cup roasted sunflower kernels
- 1 ripe avocado, sliced

POPPY SEED DRESSING:

- ¼ cup white wine vinegar
- 4 teaspoons granulated sugar
- 2 teaspoons fresh lemon juice
- ¾ teaspoon dry mustard
- Salt, to taste
- ⅔ cup vegetable oil
- 1 tablespoon poppy seed

SERVINGS
6

# Cloisonné Salad

Combine salad greens, cheese, walnuts and berries in a salad bowl. Whisk dressing ingredients until well blended. Pour dressing over salad and toss.

*Crème fraîche is the ideal addition for sauces or soups because it may be boiled without curdling. It is delicious spooned over fresh fruit or desserts such as warm cobblers or puddings. Will stay fresh in refrigerator for at least 10 days. To prepare: Combine 1 cup whipping cream and 2 tablespoons buttermilk in a glass container. Cover and let stand at room temperature until very thick, 8 to 24 hours. Stir well, then cover and chill for at least 4 hours. Variation: Whisk 1 cup heavy cream and 1 cup sour cream together in a bowl. Cover loosely with plastic wrap and let stand in a warm spot overnight, or until thickened, 8 to 24 hours. Cover and chill for at least 4 hours.*

8 cups assorted salad greens
4 ounces feta cheese, crumbled
½ cup coarsely chopped walnuts, toasted
½ cup dried raspberries, cherries or cranberries

DRESSING:
½ cup olive oil
¼ cup raspberry vinegar
½ teaspoon salt
Freshly ground black pepper
1 tablespoon crème fraîche or plain yogurt

SERVINGS
8

# Regal Romaine

Cook bacon until crisp. Drain, crumble and set aside. In a large salad bowl combine lettuce, tomatoes, cheeses, almonds and bacon. Pour dressing over salad, add croutons and toss.

Dressing: Whisk ingredients in a small bowl until well blended. Cover and let stand for 3 hours.

5 slices bacon
2 heads Romaine lettuce, torn
2 cups cherry tomatoes, cut into halves
1 cup (4 ounces) grated Swiss cheese
⅓ cup freshly grated Parmesan cheese
⅔ cup slivered almonds, toasted
1½ cups croutons

DRESSING:
4 tablespoons fresh lemon juice
3 cloves garlic, minced
Salt and freshly ground pepper, to taste
¾ cup vegetable oil

SERVINGS
8

# SUMMER CELEBRATION SALAD

Combine greens, onion, pecans, melon and grapefruit in a large salad bowl. Blend all dressing ingredients in food processor until smooth. Pour dressing over salad and toss. Garnish with blue cheese and avocado slices.

8 cups assorted salad greens
½ red onion, sliced
½ cup toasted pecans
2 cups fresh melon balls
1 grapefruit, sectioned and membranes removed
1 package (4 ounces) blue cheese, crumbled
1 ripe avocado, sliced

DRESSING:
¾ cup granulated sugar
½ cup red wine vinegar
1 teaspoon paprika
1 teaspoon salt
1 teaspoon dry mustard
1 teaspoon celery seed
1 tablespoon grated onion
Juice of ½ lemon
1 cup vegetable oil

SERVINGS
6

# SPINACH CAULIFLOWER TOSS

Cut flowerets into ¼-inch slices. Sprinkle avocado with lemon juice. In a salad bowl combine spinach, cauliflower, avocado and olives. Whisk dressing ingredients until well blended. Pour over salad, add pine nuts and toss.

½ head cauliflower, cut into flowerets
1 ripe avocado, sliced
Lemon juice
½ bunch fresh spinach, torn
½ cup small, pitted black olives
½ cup pine nuts, toasted

DRESSING:
6 tablespoons vegetable oil
3 tablespoons white wine vinegar
1 clove garlic, minced
½ teaspoon salt
½ teaspoon dry mustard
½ teaspoon dried basil
¼ teaspoon black pepper
Pinch of ground nutmeg

SERVINGS
8-10

# SALATA

Toss salad ingredients in a large salad bowl. Whisk dressing ingredients until well blended. Pour dressing over salad and toss.

1 small head romaine lettuce, torn
1 small head iceberg lettuce, torn
3 tomatoes, cut into wedges
1 small onion, thinly sliced
5 green onions, thinly sliced
5 sprigs parsley, minced
3 sprigs mint, minced
2 small cucumbers, peeled and sliced

DRESSING:

2 tablespoons olive oil
2 tablespoons vegetable oil
3 tablespoons fresh lemon juice
1 tablespoon vinegar
1 teaspoon salt
½ teaspoon black pepper
1 clove garlic, minced

The secret to staying young is to live honestly, eat slowly and lie about your age.

*Lucille Ball*

SERVINGS
6

# TABBOULEH

Cover bulgar with cold water and soak for 20 minutes. Drain, wrap in cheesecloth and squeeze to remove excess water. Place in a large bowl. Rinse and thoroughly dry parsley. In a food processor mince parsley leaves 4 cups at a time. Combine bulgar, parsley, mint, onions, tomato and cucumber in a salad bowl. Whisk together dressing ingredients and stir into salad mixture. Chill.

½ cup bulgar wheat, finely ground
8 cups fresh parsley leaves, loosely packed
¼ cup minced fresh mint
1 bunch green onions, thinly sliced
1 cup diced tomato
½ cup cucumber, peeled, seeded and diced
DRESSING:
6 tablespoons fresh lemon juice
6 tablespoons olive oil
3 tablespoons vegetable oil
1 teaspoon salt
½ teaspoon black pepper

SERVINGS
12

# GARDEN HARVEST SALAD

Cut cucumbers into quarters lengthwise then into ½-inch slices. Cut tomatoes into wedges then cut wedges in half. Combine vegetables in a large salad bowl. Whisk dressing ingredients until well blended. Pour dressing over vegetables and toss. Chill for at least 3 hours. Stir before serving.

3 pounds cucumbers, peeled
2 pounds tomatoes, peeled
1 pound green bell peppers, coarsely chopped
1 small red onion, thinly sliced
DRESSING:
1½ teaspoons salt
1½ teaspoons granulated sugar
½ cup white wine vinegar
¼ cup vegetable oil
Freshly ground pepper, to taste

SERVINGS
6

# Ensalada Cubano

Combine all ingredients and toss. Cover and let stand at room temperature for 1 hour before serving.

3 cups cooked black beans
1 red bell pepper, diced
1 yellow bell pepper, diced
3 green onions, thinly sliced
2 plum tomatoes, seeded and diced
1 package (10 ounces) frozen shoepeg corn, thawed and drained (optional)
6 tablespoons extra virgin olive oil
3 tablespoons fresh lemon juice
3 to 5 tablespoons minced fresh cilantro
1 teaspoon black pepper
Salt, to taste

SERVINGS
6-8

# Marinated Mushroom Salad

Whisk dressing ingredients until well blended. Pour dressing over vegetables and toss. Cover and chill overnight. Toss before serving.

1 pound fresh mushrooms, quartered
1 cup thinly sliced celery
½ cup diced green bell pepper
½ cup diced onion

DRESSING:

⅓ cup vegetable oil
⅓ cup olive oil
¼ cup red wine vinegar
2 teaspoons dried basil
1½ teaspoons salt
½ teaspoon granulated sugar
1 clove garlic, minced
½ teaspoon black pepper

SERVINGS
4-6

# Fresh Tomato Basil Salad

Alternate slices of tomatoes and cheese on serving platter. Sprinkle basil and onions over all. Whisk oil, vinegar, salt and pepper until well blended. Drizzle dressing over tomatoes. Garnish with basil.

- 2 pounds tomatoes, peeled and sliced
- 8 ounces mozzarella cheese, thinly sliced
- 20 fresh basil leaves, thinly sliced
- 1 bunch green onions, sliced
- ¼ cup olive oil
- 1 tablespoon balsamic vinegar
- Salt and freshly ground pepper, to taste
- Fresh basil leaves for garnish

SERVINGS
6-8

# Broccoli Raisin Salad

Cook bacon until crisp. Drain, crumble and set aside. Combine broccoli, raisins and sunflower kernels in a large bowl. In food processor combine dressing ingredients except oil. While processor is running, slowly add oil and blend on high speed for 1 minute. Pour dressing over salad, add crumbled bacon and toss to coat.

- 6 slices bacon
- 2 pounds fresh broccoli, cut into flowerets
- ½ cup raisins
- ½ cup roasted sunflower kernels

DRESSING:

- ½ medium red onion
- ¾ cup granulated sugar
- 1 teaspoon dry mustard
- 1 teaspoon salt
- ⅓ cup vinegar
- 1 cup vegetable oil

SERVINGS
4

# Marinated Asparagus

¼ cup red wine vinegar
½ cup vegetable oil
2 tablespoons Dijon mustard
½ teaspoon salt
¼ teaspoon black pepper
1 pound fresh asparagus spears, tough ends removed
1 jar (2 ounces) chopped pimiento

Whisk vinegar, oil, mustard, salt and pepper until well blended. Cook asparagus in water until crisp tender. Drain and rinse in cold water. Arrange asparagus in a 13 x 9-inch nonmetallic dish and pour marinade over top. Cover and chill for several hours or overnight. Before serving, arrange asparagus on a platter and garnish with pimiento.

A good cook is like a sorceress who dispenses happiness.

*Elsa Schiaparelli*

SERVINGS 4

# First Pick Potato Salad

Cook potatoes in boiling water until just tender, about 20 minutes. Cool. In a serving bowl combine potatoes, onion, carrot and bell pepper. Whisk dressing ingredients until well blended. Pour dressing over potato mixture and toss.

1½ pounds small red potatoes, cubed
1 small onion, diced
1 large carrot, peeled and shredded
¼ green bell pepper, diced
DRESSING:
½ cup plain yogurt, or more to taste
2 tablespoons mayonnaise
½ teaspoon granulated sugar
½ teaspoon dried tarragon
1 teaspoon caraway seed
¼ teaspoon paprika
¼ teaspoon salt
Freshly ground pepper, to taste
Ground red pepper, to taste

SERVINGS 6-8

# Wild Rice Turkey Salad

Prepare rice according to package directions. In a serving bowl toss prepared rice, turkey, peas, onion, almonds and bell pepper. Whisk dressing ingredients until well blended and stir into salad. Serve cold as a salad or warm as a main dish.

1 package (6 ounces) long-grain and wild rice mix
1 pound cooked, diced turkey
2 cups frozen peas, thawed
½ cup thinly sliced green onion
½ cup sliced almonds, toasted
¼ cup diced red bell pepper
DRESSING:
½ cup peanut oil
¼ cup tarragon vinegar
2 tablespoons Dijon mustard
1 scant tablespoon freshly grated ginger
½ teaspoon black pepper

SERVINGS
8

# ANTIPASTO SALAD

Whisk dressing ingredients until well blended. Cover and chill. Line salad bowl with lettuce leaves. Combine remaining salad ingredients, toss with dressing and spoon into salad bowl.

1 head leaf lettuce
2 tomatoes, cut into wedges
1 cup (4 ounces) grated mozzarella cheese
1 cup garbanzo beans
3 ounces thinly sliced pepperoni
1 jar (4½ ounces) marinated mushrooms, drained
1 jar (4½ ounces) marinated artichoke hearts, drained
1 jar (4½ ounces) roasted red peppers, drained
½ cup small, pitted black olives
¼ cup sliced green onions

DRESSING:
1 cup vegetable oil
¼ cup vinegar
1 clove garlic, minced
1 teaspoon salt
½ teaspoon black pepper
½ teaspoon celery salt
¼ teaspoon ground red pepper
¼ teaspoon dry mustard
Dash hot pepper sauce

**Mercifully, diets all blur together, leaving you with only one definite piece of information: french-fried potatoes are out.**

 *Jean Kerr*

SERVINGS
6

# Goat Cheese Pasta Salad

Toss pasta in a large bowl with 2 tablespoons olive oil. Cover and chill. In a small bowl combine vinegars, salt and red pepper. Whisk in remaining oil and pour over pasta. Add tomatoes, onions, olives, salami, cheese and basil. Toss to coat. Fan lettuce leaves on a platter, mound salad in center and garnish with basil leaves.

8 ounces rotini or fusilli pasta, cooked al dente and drained
½ cup olive oil, divided
¼ cup sherry vinegar
2 tablespoons balsamic vinegar
¼ teaspoon salt
¼ teaspoon crushed red pepper
4 large plum tomatoes, seeded and diced
4 green onions, thinly sliced
18 kalamata olives, pitted
4 ounces salami, sliced
2 packages (5½ ounces each) goat cheese, cut into 1½-inch pieces
½ cup fresh basil leaves, thinly sliced
Red leaf lettuce leaves
Fresh basil leaves for garnish

SERVINGS
6

# Greek Pasta Salad

Toss pasta with cheese and pine nuts in a salad bowl. Stir in garlic, rosemary, oil and lemon juice. Cover and chill. Serve pasta surrounded with olives.

8 ounces orzo pasta, cooked al dente and drained
1 cup feta cheese, crumbled
1 cup pine nuts, toasted
2 cloves garlic, minced
¼ cup minced fresh rosemary
¼ cup olive oil
Juice of 1 lemon
1 cup pitted nicoise olives for garnish

SERVINGS
6

# PASTA PECAN SALAD

Toss pasta, ham, parsley, rosemary, oil, vinegar, garlic and pepper. Cover and chill for several hours or overnight. About 30 minutes before serving, toss pasta mixture with pecans, blue cheese and Parmesan cheese.

- 3 cups farfalle pasta, cooked al dente and drained
- 4 ounces cooked ham, cut into strips
- 1/3 cup minced fresh parsley
- 2 tablespoons minced fresh rosemary
- 1/4 cup olive oil
- 2 tablespoons raspberry vinegar
- 1 clove garlic, minced
- 1/2 teaspoon coarsely ground black pepper
- 1 cup coarsely chopped pecans, toasted
- 1 package (4 ounces) blue cheese, crumbled
- 1/3 cup freshly grated Parmesan cheese

**Laughter is brightest where food is best.**

*Irish Proverb*

SERVINGS
4

# FIESTA CHICKEN SALAD

Pour 1 cup dressing over chicken, cover and chill for 2 hours. Combine bell peppers, hearts of palm, tomatillos, beans and corn in a large bowl and toss with remaining dressing. Grill chicken over hot coals until done, 10 to 15 minutes. Cut each breast into 4 strips. Arrange 2 radicchio and 2 lettuce leaves on each salad plate. Spoon vegetables over lettuce and top with grilled chicken.

Dressing: Combine cilantro, basil, thyme, shallots and garlic in a small bowl. Add vinegars and wine. Slowly whisk in oils, salt and pepper.

4 chicken breast halves, skinned and boned
½ cup diced red bell pepper
½ cup diced green bell pepper
½ cup sliced hearts of palm
½ cup tomatillos, husked and diced
½ cup cooked black beans
½ cup fresh corn, cooked

DRESSING:
¼ cup minced fresh cilantro
¼ cup minced fresh basil
2 tablespoons minced fresh thyme
4 shallots, minced
2 cloves garlic, minced
2 tablespoons white wine vinegar
¼ cup balsamic vinegar
2 tablespoons dry white wine
½ cup olive oil
½ cup vegetable oil
½ teaspoon salt
Freshly ground pepper, to taste

GARNISH:
8 large radicchio leaves
8 large leaf lettuce leaves

SERVINGS
5

# ORIENTAL CHICKEN SALAD

Place chicken, green onions and ginger in a large saucepan and cover with water. Simmer until thoroughly cooked, 20 to 30 minutes. Drain, discarding onions and ginger. Cool chicken, cut into bite-size pieces and place in a large bowl. Add noodles, snow peas, water chestnuts, green onions and bell pepper. Pour dressing over salad and toss. Cover and chill for 24 hours. Before serving, sprinkle with almonds and sesame seed.

Dressing: In a small bowl whisk vinegar, sugar and salt until sugar is dissolved. Add sesame oil, vegetable oil and pepper and whisk until well blended.

4 chicken breast halves, skinned and boned
2 green onions, cut in 2-inch slices
1 slice fresh ginger (¼-inch)
5 ounces Chinese noodles, cooked and drained
1 cup snow peas, sliced lengthwise
1 can (8 ounces) sliced water chestnuts
2 green onions, thinly sliced
½ cup sliced red bell pepper
3 tablespoons sliced almonds, toasted
1½ tablespoons sesame seed, toasted

DRESSING:
4 tablespoons rice vinegar
2 tablespoons granulated sugar
½ teaspoon salt
3 tablespoons dark sesame oil
1 tablespoon vegetable oil
¼ teaspoon black pepper

I know God will not give me anything I can't handle. I just wish He didn't trust me so much.

*Mother Teresa*

SERVINGS
4

# CHICKEN CAESAR SALAD

Whisk marinade ingredients, blending well. Pour over chicken and chill for several hours. Grill chicken over medium coals until done, 10 to 15 minutes. Cut into 1-inch strips.

Pour dressing over lettuce and toss. Add cheese and pepper and toss again. Serve on individual salad plates topped with sliced, grilled chicken.

Dressing: In a food processor combine mayonnaise, mustard, garlic, lemon juice, vinegar, Worcestershire sauce, anchovy paste and hot pepper sauce until well blended. With processor running, add oil in a steady stream.

4 chicken breast halves, skinned and boned
1 head romaine lettuce, torn
⅓ cup freshly grated Parmesan cheese
Freshly ground black pepper, to taste

MARINADE:
3 tablespoons fresh lemon juice
2 tablespoons Worcestershire sauce
¼ cup dry white wine
3 tablespoons vegetable oil
¼ teaspoon black pepper
1 tablespoon minced fresh parsley
¼ teaspoon salt
¼ teaspoon dried oregano

DRESSING:
½ cup mayonnaise
1½ tablespoons dry mustard
4 or 5 cloves garlic, minced
1½ tablespoons fresh lemon juice
1 tablespoon red wine vinegar
1 tablespoon Worcestershire sauce
1 tablespoon anchovy paste
6 drops hot pepper sauce
¾ cup vegetable oil

SERVINGS
8-10

# Carmen Miranda Chicken Salad

Whisk together dressing ingredients. Pour over chicken and let stand for 30 minutes. Stir in wild rice, snow peas, pineapple, orange slices and almonds. Chill for 2 hours. Before serving, gently stir in kiwi fruit.

5 cups cooked, diced chicken
2 cups cooked wild rice
1½ cups snow peas, blanched
2 cups fresh pineapple chunks
2 cups orange slices
¾ cup slivered almonds, toasted
5 kiwi fruit, peeled and sliced
DRESSING:
¼ cup vegetable oil
¼ cup orange juice
¼ cup vinegar
¼ cup honey
1 tablespoon Dijon mustard
1 teaspoon salt

Chicken salad has a certain glamour about it. Like the little black dress, it is chic and acceptable anywhere.

*Laurie Colwin*

SERVINGS
6

# Madras Chicken Salad

Toss chicken, cabbage, bell pepper and pickle in a medium bowl. Combine dressing ingredients, pour over chicken mixture and toss. Serve chutney and dry roasted peanuts on the side.

**4 cups cooked, diced chicken**
**1½ cups shredded cabbage**
**1 green bell pepper, sliced**
**1 large dill pickle, diced**
**¾ cup chutney**
**¾ cup dry roasted peanuts**
**Dressing:**
**2 cloves garlic, minced**
**¼ cup capers, with liquid**
**3 tablespoons malt vinegar**
**6 tablespoons mayonnaise**
**1 to 2 tablespoons Madras curry powder**
**3 tablespoons sour cream**

SERVINGS
10-12

# Shrimp Pasta Salad

Sauté bell peppers in oil over medium heat for five minutes. Pour peppers and oil over pasta in a large bowl. Drain artichoke liquid into pasta. Slice artichoke hearts in half and add to pasta with remaining ingredients. Toss well, cover and chill for several hours or overnight.

**½ cup diced red bell pepper**
**½ cup diced green bell pepper**
**⅓ cup vegetable oil**
**12 ounces shell pasta, cooked al dente and drained**
**2 jars (6 ounces each) marinated artichoke hearts, with liquid**
**1 pound shrimp, cooked and deveined**
**¼ pound fresh mushrooms, sliced**
**1 cup diced tomatoes**
**1 cup sliced celery**
**⅓ cup fresh lemon juice**
**1 cup small pitted black olives**
**½ cup minced fresh parsley**
**1 tablespoon dried Italian seasonings**
**Salt and pepper, to taste**

SERVINGS
6-8

# CEVICHE

Combine shrimp, onion, chili pepper and tomato in a salad bowl. Whisk dressing ingredients until well blended. Pour over shrimp mixture, cover and chill for at least 4 hours. Before serving, stir beer into shrimp mixture. Serve over salad greens.

*For authentic Latin American flavor, garnish with popped popcorn.*

- 2 pounds shrimp, cooked and deveined
- 1 medium white onion, diced
- 1 Anaheim chili pepper, seeded and diced
- 1 tomato, peeled, seeded and diced
- ½ cup beer
- 4 cups assorted salad greens

DRESSING:

- Juice of 1 lemon
- ½ cup ketchup
- 2 tablespoons frozen orange juice concentrate
- 2 tablespoons minced fresh cilantro
- 1 teaspoon granulated sugar
- Salt and pepper, to taste

SERVINGS
6

# CURRIED SALMON SALAD

Combine mayonnaise, lime juice, chutney, curry powder, salt and pepper in a small bowl. Mix salmon, cucumber, onion and parsley in another bowl and toss gently with mayonnaise mixture. Core each tomato and cut three-fourths of the way down to form eight wedge-shaped petals. Fill the center with salmon salad. Serve on a bed of lettuce garnished with lemon wedges and mint sprigs.

- 2 tablespoons mayonnaise
- 3 tablespoons fresh lime juice
- 3 tablespoons chopped chutney
- ½ teaspoon curry powder
- Salt and freshly ground pepper, to taste
- 2 cups flaked freshly cooked salmon
- 1 medium cucumber, peeled and chopped
- 1 green onion, thinly sliced
- 2 tablespoons minced fresh parsley
- 6 large tomatoes
- Lettuce leaves
- Lemon wedges for garnish
- Mint sprigs for garnish

SERVINGS
6

# Shrimp Salad Caribe

Combine shrimp, beans, bell pepper, celery, jícama and onion in large bowl. Mix dressing ingredients and pour over shrimp mixture, tossing lightly to coat. Cover and chill for 2 hours, stirring occasionally. Spoon salad onto a lettuce-lined platter or individual salad plates and garnish with tomatoes.

1 pound medium shrimp, cooked and deveined
1 can (15 ounces) black beans, rinsed and drained
1 small green bell pepper, julienned
½ cup thinly sliced celery
½ cup jícama, julienned
½ small red onion, thinly sliced
Lettuce leaves
1 cup cherry tomatoes, cut into halves for garnish
DRESSING:
⅔ cup picante sauce
2 tablespoons minced fresh cilantro
2 tablespoons honey
2 tablespoons vegetable oil
2 tablespoons fresh lime juice
1 teaspoon lime zest
½ teaspoon salt

SERVINGS
1 cup

# Pecan Garlic Dressing

Combine garlic, sugar, salt and pepper in food processor. Scrape down sides and add vinegar. Pulse 3 or 4 times. While food processor is running, add olive oil in a steady stream and process until well blended. Stir in pecans and serve with assorted salad greens.

3 large cloves garlic
½ teaspoon granulated sugar
½ teaspoon salt
¼ teaspoon freshly ground pepper
¼ cup red wine vinegar
¾ cup olive oil
¼ cup coarsely chopped pecans, toasted

SERVINGS

1¼ cups

# PEPPER CREAM DRESSING

- 1 cup mayonnaise
- 2 tablespoons water
- ½ teaspoon lemon juice
- ¾ teaspoon Worcestershire sauce
- ¾ teaspoon dry mustard
- 1 tablespoon freshly ground pepper
- ¾ teaspoon garlic salt
- ¼ cup freshly grated Parmesan cheese

Combine all ingredients in food processor until well blended. Cover and chill.

**A little of what you fancy does you good.**

*Marie Lloyd*

SERVINGS
¾ cup

# Citrus Spa Vinaigrette

Combine water, vinegar and cornstarch in a small saucepan. Bring to a boil and cook, stirring constantly for 1 minute. Remove from heat and set aside. Combine garlic and salt in a bowl. Mash with back of a spoon to make a paste. Stir into cornstarch mixture with basil, orange zest and oil. Cover and chill. Serve with assorted salad greens.

- ½ cup cold water
- 2 tablespoons white wine vinegar
- 1 tablespoon cornstarch
- 1 clove garlic, minced
- ⅛ teaspoon salt
- 1 teaspoon minced fresh basil
- ¼ teaspoon grated orange zest
- 1 teaspoon olive oil

SERVINGS
10-12

# Cranberry Almond Relish

Bring water to a boil, stir in sugar and boil for 5 minutes. Add cranberries and cook until they become transparent and pop. Remove from heat and stir in marmalade and lemon juice. Cool mixture for 20 to 30 minutes then chill for several hours. Stir in almonds when relish is well chilled.

- 1 cup water
- 2 cups granulated sugar
- 1 pound fresh cranberries
- 1 jar (10 ounces) orange marmalade
- Juice of 2 lemons
- ⅔ cup slivered almonds, toasted

SERVINGS
18

# Spiced Peaches

Combine vinegar, sugar, water, cinnamon, allspice and ginger in a large saucepan. Bring to a boil, reduce heat and simmer until sugar dissolves. Simmer for 20 minutes to blend flavors. Add peaches and cool to room temperature. Cover and chill for at least 2 days before serving.

2 cups rice wine vinegar
1 cup granulated sugar
1 cup water
1 cinnamon stick
1 teaspoon whole allspice
1 ounce fresh ginger, peeled and sliced thin
18 canned peach halves, drained and rinsed

SERVINGS
16

# Tutti Frutti

Combine apples, oranges, pineapple and cantalope in a large bowl. Pour marinade over fruit. Cover and chill for several hours or overnight. Before serving, stir in strawberries and garnish with mint leaves.

Marinade: Combine sugar, water, lemon juice and cinnamon sticks in a medium saucepan. Tie cloves and allspice in cheesecloth and add to mixture. Boil until sugar is dissolved. Reduce heat, cover and simmer for 5 minutes. Remove from heat and cool. Remove cinnamon sticks and spice bag. Stir in kirsch.

3 large apples, peeled and cubed
3 large oranges, sectioned
1 small pineapple, cut into wedges
1 small cantaloupe, cut into wedges
1 pint strawberries, sliced
Mint leaves for garnish
MARINADE:
½ cup granulated sugar
1 cup water
½ teaspoon lemon juice
2 cinnamon sticks
½ teaspoon whole cloves
½ teaspoon whole allspice
½ cup kirsch liqueur

# GIVE US YOUR HUNGRY MASSES

## "What we have in mind is brunch for 200 million people!"

A gift to the American people from the food-loving folk of France, maybe the Statue of Liberty should be holding a giant sourdough baguette instead of a torch. ❖ Because to the rest of the world, America was the Land of the Big Loaf, fresh and crusty and just waiting to be buttered. ❖ "Come on over for brunch," Lady Liberty seemed to call to the world. "And bring your cousins! There's alway's room to set another plate at America's table." ❖ The Statue also told people looking for a new start that America loves its huddled masses. Masses huddled over big baskets of blueberry muffins, masses huddled around tables laden with all the good things harvested from freedom's bounty. The fruit of America's land and labors. ❖ Today, the Statue of Liberty is still the symbol of America's opportunity and hospitality. So the next time you bake a loaf of bread, bake one for a neighbor. Or invite an extra mouth or two to your next bountiful brunch. Her "world-wide welcome" is a promise she made many years ago and a promise that's still a pleasure to keep.

Breads & Brunches

SERVINGS

24-30 pancakes

# Painted Porch Pancakes

Combine flours, oats, cornmeal, baking powder, baking soda and salt in a food processor. Add butter and process until mixture resembles coarse meal. In a large bowl beat eggs and buttermilk. Add honey and mix well. Stir in dry ingredients and fold in pecans. Pour ¼ cup batter onto lightly oiled, preheated griddle. When pancakes bubble, turn and cook until golden. (Pancakes may be kept warm in a 200 degree oven until ready to serve.) Serve with butter and warm syrup or fresh fruit.

*Note: Batter may be made ahead and refrigerated overnight.*

- 1½ cups whole-wheat flour
- 1 cup all-purpose flour
- 1 cup rolled oats
- ½ cup yellow cornmeal
- 1 tablespoon baking powder
- 2 teaspoons baking soda
- 1 teaspoon salt
- ¾ cup unsalted butter, chilled and sliced
- 4 eggs
- 4 cups buttermilk
- ½ cup honey
- 1 cup chopped pecans

4

# Prairie Puffcake

Mix eggs, flour, 1 tablespoon sugar, baking powder, salt and milk until smooth. Add 2 tablespoons melted butter and vanilla. Set aside for 30 minutes or chill overnight.

Preheat oven to 425 degrees. In a small bowl combine sugar, cinnamon and nutmeg. Melt 2 tablespoons butter in a 10-inch ovenproof skillet. Sprinkle ⅓ cup of the sugar mixture over butter. Arrange apple slices in skillet and sprinkle with remaining sugar. Cook over medium heat until mixture bubbles. Remove from heat and pour batter over apples. Bake on center rack for 15 minutes. Reduce heat to 375 degrees and bake for 10 minutes. Invert onto serving platter and dust with confectioners' sugar. (Pancake will fall.) Cut into wedges. Serve immediately with warm syrup.

- 5 large eggs, lightly beaten
- ½ cup all-purpose flour
- 1 tablespoon granulated sugar
- ½ teaspoon baking powder
- Pinch of salt
- 1 cup milk
- ¼ cup butter, divided
- 1 teaspoon vanilla extract
- ⅔ cup granulated sugar
- ½ teaspoon ground cinnamon
- ¼ teaspoon freshly grated nutmeg
- 1 large tart apple, peeled and thinly sliced
- Confectioners' sugar, for garnish

SERVINGS
12-15

# BAKED CRAB FONDUE

Butter two 13 x 9-inch baking dishes. Remove crust from bread and discard. Tear bread into small pieces. Set aside to dry for 2 hours. Divide bread between prepared pans and drizzle with melted butter. Arrange crabmeat and cheeses over bread. Beat eggs, milk, wine, mustard, black pepper and white pepper in a large bowl. Stir in onions and pour over crabmeat. Cover and chill overnight.

Preheat oven to 325 degrees. Arrange tomatoes on top, cover and bake for 50 minutes. Spread with sour cream and sprinkle with Parmesan cheese. Bake uncovered until cheese melts and top is crusty, 10 to 15 minutes.

1 loaf (16 ounces) French bread
6 tablespoons butter, melted
12 ounces cooked crabmeat, shredded
3 cups (12 ounces) grated Swiss cheese
2 cups (8 ounces) grated Monterey Jack cheese
16 eggs
3¼ cups milk
½ cup white wine – sherry
1 tablespoon Dijon mustard
¼ teaspoon black pepper
⅛ teaspoon white pepper
4 green onions, sliced
TOPPING:
4 plum tomatoes, thinly sliced
1½ cups sour cream
⅔ cup freshly grated Parmesan cheese

After all, tomorrow is another day.

*Margaret Mitchell*

SERVINGS
12

# FIESTA EGG CASSEROLE

Preheat oven to 350 degrees. Butter a 13 x 9-inch casserole dish. Beat eggs in a large bowl. Stir in cheeses, add remaining ingredients and mix well. Pour into prepared dish. Bake until edges are golden brown and center is set, 35 to 45 minutes. Serve with Salsa Fresca (page 32).

- 10 eggs
- 2 cups (8 ounces) grated Monterey Jack cheese
- 2 cups (8 ounces) grated cheddar cheese
- 2 cups small-curd cottage cheese
- 2 cans (4½ ounces each) chopped green chilies
- ½ cup butter, melted
- ½ cup all-purpose flour
- 1 teaspoon baking powder
- ½ teaspoon salt

SERVINGS
8

# CALIFORNIA STRATA

Butter a 13 x 9-inch casserole dish. Sauté mushrooms and onion in butter until tender, 5 to 8 minutes. Season with salt and pepper and remove from pan. Crumble sausage into skillet and cook until no longer pink. Drain well. Place 6 slices of bread in bottom of prepared dish and layer half the mushroom mixture, sausage and cheese. Repeat layers ending with cheese. Beat eggs, milk, mustards, nutmeg, salt and pepper. Pour over casserole. Cover and chill overnight.

Preheat oven to 350 degrees. Sprinkle parsley over top and bake uncovered until bubbly, 1 hour.

- ½ pound fresh mushrooms, sliced
- 1 cup diced yellow onion
- ¼ cup butter
- Salt and freshly ground pepper, to taste
- 1 pound mild Italian sausage
- 12 slices white bread, crusts removed
- 3 cups (12 ounces) grated cheddar cheese
- 5 eggs
- 2½ cups milk
- 1 tablespoon Dijon mustard
- 1 teaspoon dry mustard
- 1 teaspoon ground nutmeg
- 1 teaspoon salt
- ⅛ teaspoon black pepper
- 1 tablespoon minced fresh parsley

SERVINGS 6

# QUESO QUICHE WITH AVOCADO SALSA

Preheat oven to 400 degrees. Bake pie crust for 7 minutes, remove from oven and reduce heat to 375 degrees. Brown ground beef, onion, green chilies and taco seasoning. Drain. Sprinkle cheese over bottom of pie crust and spread with beef mixture. Beat eggs, half-and-half, salt and pepper. Pour over pie. Bake until a knife inserted off-center comes out clean, 45 minutes. Let stand for 10 minutes before cutting. Serve with Avocado Salsa, shredded lettuce and tomatoes on the side.

Avocado Salsa: Combine all ingredients, cover and chill.

Crust for a 9-inch deep-dish pie
½ pound ground beef
¼ cup diced onion
1 can (4½ ounces) chopped green chilies
2 tablespoons taco seasoning mix
1½ cups (6 ounces) grated cheddar cheese
3 eggs
1½ cups half-and-half
½ teaspoon salt
⅛ teaspoon black pepper
Shredded lettuce
Diced tomatoes
AVOCADO SALSA:
2 ripe avocados, mashed
1 clove garlic, minced
3 tablespoons fresh lemon juice
1 tomato, diced
1 jalapeño pepper, seeded and minced (optional)

SERVINGS 6

# CREAM CHEESE EGGS

Cook bacon until crisp. Drain, crumble and set aside. In a large skillet sauté onion and bell pepper in butter until tender, 5 to 8 minutes. Combine eggs, milk, seasonings, cream cheese and tomato. Pour over onions and peppers. Cook eggs, pushing them with a spatula across bottom and sides of skillet, forming large curds. Remove from heat while eggs are still moist. Do not overcook. Sprinkle with bacon and serve immediately.

4 slices bacon
½ cup diced onion
½ cup diced green bell pepper
2 tablespoons butter
8 eggs, lightly beaten
¼ cup milk
1 teaspoon seasoned salt
½ teaspoon dried basil
¼ teaspoon seasoned pepper
1 package (3 ounces) cream cheese, cubed
1 medium tomato, diced

SERVINGS 6

# TOMATO CHEESE PIE

Preheat oven to 375 degrees. Brush baked pie crust with Dijon mustard and set aside. Combine flour, salt and pepper. Dredge tomatoes in flour mixture, sauté for 3 minutes in butter and drain. Layer tomatoes, olives and onions in pie crust. Combine cheeses and sprinkle over top. In a medium bowl mix eggs, cream and seasonings and pour over pie. Sprinkle with paprika. Bake until set, 40 to 45 minutes. Let stand for 5 to 10 minutes before cutting.

- Crust for a 9-inch deep-dish pie, baked
- ½ tablespoon Dijon mustard
- ¼ cup all-purpose flour
- ½ teaspoon salt
- ⅛ teaspoon black pepper
- 2 ripe tomatoes, peeled and sliced ½ inch thick
- 2 tablespoons butter
- ¼ cup sliced black olives
- 1 bunch green onions, sliced
- ½ cup (2 ounces) grated Provolone cheese
- ¾ cup (3 ounces) grated cheddar cheese
- 2 eggs, lightly beaten
- 1 cup heavy cream
- ½ teaspoon salt
- ⅛ teaspoon black pepper
- ⅛ teaspoon ground nutmeg
- Pinch of ground red pepper
- Paprika

SERVINGS 5

# MAGNIFICENT MUSHROOMS

Sauté onions in butter for 2 to 3 minutes in a large skillet. Add mushrooms, paprika, salt and pepper and continue cooking until mushrooms are tender. Stir in sour cream and heat thoroughly. (May be refrigerated overnight at this point.) Wrap Canadian bacon in foil and heat. Place slice of bacon on each muffin half and spoon warm mushroom sauce over top. Serve immediately.

- ¼ cup sliced green onion tops
- ½ cup butter
- 1 pound fresh mushrooms, sliced
- 1 teaspoon paprika
- ½ teaspoon salt
- Freshly ground pepper, to taste
- 2 cups sour cream
- 10 slices Canadian bacon
- 5 English muffins, split and toasted

SERVINGS
6-8

# ROMA CHEESE SOUFFLÉS

Butter bread slices and cut into small cubes. In a medium bowl combine eggs, cheese, mustard, red pepper, salt, Worcestershire sauce and milk. Stir in bread and chill for several hours or overnight.

Preheat oven to 350 degrees. Cut a sliver off bottom of each tomato to make it stand upright. Slice top off each tomato and carefully remove pulp and seeds. Invert on paper towel to drain. Brush inside of each tomato with olive oil and sprinkle with basil. Fill with cheese mixture and place in a baking dish. Bake until puffy and golden, 20 minutes. Serve immediately.

- 6 slices white bread, crusts removed
- ¼ cup butter, softened
- 3 eggs, beaten
- 1½ cups (6 ounces) grated sharp cheddar cheese
- ½ teaspoon dry mustard
- Pinch of ground red pepper
- ½ teaspoon salt
- Dash Worcestershire sauce
- 1 cup milk
- 12 plum tomatoes
- Olive oil
- 1 teaspoon dried basil

Progress in civilization has been accompanied by progress in cookery.

*Fannie Farmer*

SERVINGS
20 pieces

# CHICKEN TRIANGLES

1 cup butter, divided
8 chicken breast halves, skinned, boned and diced
1 pound fresh mushrooms, sliced
1 bunch green onions, sliced
½ cup diced shallots
¼ cup all-purpose flour
2 cups heavy cream
1 cup white wine
½ cup Dijon mustard
1 teaspoon dried tarragon
½ teaspoon salt
½ teaspoon black pepper
1 package (16 ounces) frozen phyllo dough, thawed

Melt ½ cup butter in a large skillet and sauté chicken until lightly browned. Remove with a slotted spoon and set aside. Sauté mushrooms, onions and shallots in drippings until onions are tender, 5 to 8 minutes. Sprinkle flour over mushroom mixture and stir for 2 minutes. Add cream and bring to a boil. Cook, stirring constantly until smooth. Add wine, mustard and seasonings. Cook until thick. Stir in chicken, cover and chill.

Preheat oven to 400 degrees. Line a baking sheet with parchment paper or foil. Melt remaining ½ cup butter. Unroll phyllo dough and remove 3 sheets. Cover unused dough with plastic wrap to keep sheets from drying out. Brush each sheet lightly with melted butter and stack one on top of the other. Cut stack into 3 strips, about 4x18 inches. Place ¼ cup of chicken mixture at end of each strip. Fold corner over diagonally to form a triangle. Fold flag-fashion to opposite end. Brush top of each triangle with melted butter. Place on prepared baking sheet. Repeat process until all dough is used. Bake until light golden brown, 20 minutes.

*Triangles may be frozen on a baking sheet then placed in an airtight container. Bake until light golden brown, 20 to 30 minutes.*

SERVINGS
24 crêpes

# SAUSAGE CRÊPES

**Crêpes:**
1 cup cold water
1 cup cold milk
4 eggs
½ teaspoon salt
2 cups all-purpose flour
¼ cup butter, melted

**Filling:**
2 pounds bulk sausage
½ cup diced onion
1 cup grated cheddar cheese
2 packages (3 ounces each) cream cheese
¼ teaspoon dried marjoram

**Topping:**
½ cup butter, softened
1 cup sour cream

Blend all ingredients in food processor until smooth. Chill batter for at least 2 hours. Brush a 6-inch crêpe pan or iron skillet with oil and heat on medium-high until very hot. Pour 2 tablespoons batter in pan and tilt in all directions so batter is spread evenly over bottom. Return pan to heat for 1 minute. Turn crêpe when bottom is lightly browned and cook other side for 30 seconds. Slide from pan onto waxed paper. Repeat with remaining batter.

Fill each crêpe with 2 tablespoons filling. Roll up and place seam side down in prepared dish. Bake for 20 minutes. Spread topping over crêpes and bake for an additional 5 minutes

Filling: Preheat oven to 325 degrees. Butter two 13 x 9-inch casserole dishes. Brown sausage with onion and drain. Add cheddar cheese, cream cheese and marjoram. Mix well.

Topping: Combine butter and sour cream until smooth.

*Crêpes may be used immediately, refrigerated overnight or frozen for up to 3 months. To freeze, stack cooled crêpes between waxed paper and wrap in foil. Thaw at room temperature for 1 hour.*

SERVINGS
16 crêpes

# CHICKEN CRÊPES

Blend all crêpe ingredients in food processor until smooth. Set batter aside for 2 to 3 hours or cover and chill for up to 12 hours. Brush a 6-inch crêpe pan or iron skillet with oil and heat on medium-high until very hot. Pour 2 tablespoons of batter in pan and tilt in all directions so batter is spread evenly over bottom. Return to heat for 1 minute. Turn crêpe when bottom is lightly browned and cook other side for 30 seconds. Slide from pan onto waxed paper. Repeat with remaining batter. Crêpes may be used immediately, refrigerated overnight or frozen for up to 3 months. To freeze, stack cooled crêpes between waxed paper and wrap in foil. Thaw at room temperature for 1 hour. Makes 16 to 18 crêpes.

Preheat oven to 350 degrees. Butter two 13 x 9-inch casserole dishes. Fill each crêpe with 3 tablespoons filling. Roll up and place seam side down in prepared dish. (Crêpes may be frozen at this point. If frozen, bring to room temperature before topping with sauce.) Spoon 1 cup sauce over each pan. Bake for 15 minutes. Serve remaining sauce on the side.

Filling: Drain spinach and squeeze dry. Sauté onion in butter until tender, 5 to 8 minutes. Add mushrooms and sauté for 4 minutes. Remove from heat and add spinach, chicken, sour cream, sherry and salt. Stir until well blended. This filling may be prepared ahead and chilled.

Sauce: Combine butter and flour until smooth. Stir in sherry, chicken broth and milk. Bring to a boil, stirring constantly. Reduce heat and simmer for 5 minutes. Add cheeses and salt and stir over low heat until melted. Remove from heat and cover with waxed paper directly on sauce.

**CRÊPES:**
**3 eggs**
**Pinch of salt**
**1¼ cups beer, room temperature**
**1 cup less 2 tablespoons all-purpose flour**
**¼ cup butter, melted**
**FILLING:**
**½ package (10 ounces) frozen chopped spinach, thawed**
**1 medium onion, diced**
**¼ cup butter**
**½ pound fresh mushrooms, sliced**
**2 cups cooked, diced chicken**
**6 tablespoons sour cream**
**2 tablespoons dry sherry**
**Salt, to taste**
**SAUCE:**
**6 tablespoons butter, melted**
**6 tablespoons all-purpose flour**
**½ cup dry sherry**
**2 cups chicken broth**
**1 cup milk**
**¾ cup freshly grated Parmesan cheese**
**½ cup (2 ounces) grated Swiss cheese**
**Salt, to taste**

SERVINGS
2 cups

# GRAND MARNIER CRÈME

Beat cream cheese, marshmallow cream and Grand Marnier until smooth. Pour into a serving bowl and sprinkle with brown sugar. Serve as a dip with assorted fresh fruit. Strawberries, sliced peaches and pears are especially good with this dip. Toss sliced fruit with one tablespoon lemon juice and two tablespoons water.

1 package (8 ounces) cream cheese, softened
1 jar (7 ounces) marshmallow cream
¼ cup Grand Marnier liqueur
2 tablespoons packed brown sugar
Fresh fruit

If you want the rainbow,
you gotta put up
with the rain.

*Dolly Parton*

SERVINGS
8

# Plum Coffee Cake

Preheat oven to 450 degrees. Butter a 9-inch springform pan. Cream butter and sugar in a large mixing bowl. Add eggs and blend well. Combine flour, baking powder, cinnamon and salt. In a small bowl combine milk, almond extract and vanilla. Add dry mixture and milk alternately to creamed mixture in thirds. Pour into prepared pan. Arrange plums on top of batter. Sprinkle with topping and bake for 30 to 35 minutes. Serve immediately.

Topping: Mix flour, sugar and butter with fork until crumbly. Stir in almonds.

*If fresh plums are not in season, 2 cups canned plums may be substituted.*

½ cup butter, softened
½ cup granulated sugar
2 eggs
1 cup all-purpose flour
1 teaspoon baking powder
1 teaspoon ground cinnamon
¼ teaspoon salt
⅓ cup milk
1 teaspoon almond extract
½ teaspoon vanilla extract
1½ pounds fresh plums, pitted and quartered

TOPPING:
1 tablespoon all-purpose flour
2 tablespoons granulated sugar
1 tablespoon butter
¼ cup slivered almonds, toasted

SERVINGS
12-15

# Raisin Nut Crumb Cake

Preheat oven to 350 degrees. Grease a 13 x 9-inch cake pan. Combine flour, sugar, butter and brown sugar until crumbly. Reserve ¾ cup for topping. To remaining mixture add cinnamon, nutmeg, salt, allspice and cloves. Stir in buttermilk, eggs, baking soda, raisins and nuts and mix well. Pour into prepared pan. Sprinkle reserved crumb mixture over top. Bake for 35 to 40 minutes or until wooden toothpick inserted in center comes out clean.

3 cups all-purpose flour
2 cups granulated sugar
1 cup butter, softened
¼ cup packed brown sugar
1 teaspoon ground cinnamon
1 teaspoon ground nutmeg
½ teaspoon salt
½ teaspoon ground allspice
½ teaspoon ground cloves
2 cups buttermilk
2 eggs, beaten
2 teaspoons baking soda
1 cup raisins
1 cup chopped pecans or walnuts

SERVINGS
10-12

# Raspberry Cream Cheese Coffee Cake

Preheat oven to 350 degrees. Grease and flour bottom and sides of 10-inch springform pan. In a large bowl combine flour and ¾ cup sugar. Use a pastry blender or fork to cut in butter until mixture resembles coarse crumbs. Reserve 1 cup for topping. Combine remaining crumb mixture with sour cream, 1 egg, almond extract, baking soda, baking powder and salt. Spread dough over bottom and 2 inches up the sides of prepared pan. Beat cream cheese, ¼ cup sugar and 1 egg until blended. Spread over dough. Spoon preserves evenly over cheese filling. Combine reserved crumb mixture and almonds and sprinkle over top. Bake until cheese filling is set and crust is a deep golden brown, 45 to 55 minutes. Cool for 15 minutes, remove sides of pan and cut cake into wedges.

**2¼ cups all-purpose flour**
**1 cup granulated sugar, divided**
**¾ cup butter or margarine, softened**
**¾ cup sour cream**
**2 eggs**
**1 teaspoon almond extract**
**½ teaspoon baking soda**
**½ teaspoon baking powder**
**¼ teaspoon salt**
**1 package (8 ounces) cream cheese, softened**
**½ cup raspberry preserves**
**½ cup sliced almonds**

SERVINGS
24 muffins

# Am-I-Blue Berry Muffins

Preheat oven to 400 degrees. Grease two 12-count muffin pans. In a large bowl combine flour, sugar, baking powder and salt. Cut in butter until mixture resembles fine crumbs. In a small bowl beat eggs, milk and vanilla. Stir into flour mixture until just moistened. Gently fold in blueberries. Spoon batter into prepared pans. Bake until golden brown, 20 minutes. Cool on a wire rack for 5 minutes before removing from pan.

**2½ cups all-purpose flour**
**¾ cup granulated sugar**
**1 tablespoon baking powder**
**½ teaspoon salt**
**6 tablespoons butter**
**2 eggs**
**1 cup milk**
**1 teaspoon vanilla extract**
**1½ cups fresh or frozen blueberries**

SERVINGS
24 muffins

# Apple Crisp Muffins

Preheat oven to 350 degrees. Grease and flour two 12-count muffin pans or use paper liners. In a large bowl combine flour, apples, sugar, salt, baking soda and cinnamon. Stir in oil, eggs, pecans and vanilla. (Batter will resemble cookie dough.) Fill muffin cups to top. Bake for 30 minutes. Cool on a wire rack for 5 minutes before removing from pan. Serve warm.

**3½ cups all-purpose flour**
**3 cups peeled, diced apples**
**2 cups granulated sugar**
**1 teaspoon salt**
**1 teaspoon baking soda**
**1 teaspoon ground cinnamon**
**1¼ cups vegetable oil**
**2 eggs, lightly beaten**
**½ cup chopped pecans or walnuts**
**1 teaspoon vanilla extract**

SERVINGS
16 muffins

# Raspberry Almond Muffins

Preheat oven to 350 degrees. Place foil baking liners in 16 muffin cups. Cut almond paste into 16 pieces. Pat each piece into a 1½-inch circle and set aside. Cream butter and sugar in a large bowl until fluffy. Beat in eggs, one at a time. Stir in baking powder, baking soda and almond extract. Fold in 1 cup flour, then yogurt, then remaining flour. Spoon 2 tablespoons of batter into each muffin cup. Top each with 1 tablespoon of preserves. Press 1 piece of almond paste into preserves and top with 2 tablespoons of batter. Bake until lightly browned, 25 to 30 minutes. Remove from pan and cool on a wire rack for 10 minutes.

**5 ounces almond paste**
**½ cup butter, softened**
**¾ cup granulated sugar**
**2 large eggs**
**1 teaspoon baking powder**
**½ teaspoon baking soda**
**1 teaspoon almond extract**
**2 cups all-purpose flour**
**1 cup plain yogurt**
**¾ cup raspberry preserves**

SERVINGS
24 muffins

# POPPY SEED MUFFINS WITH ALMOND GLAZE

Preheat oven to 350 degrees. Grease two 12-count muffin pans. In a large bowl combine flour, sugar, baking powder and salt. Add remaining ingredients and beat with an electric mixer on high for two minutes. Fill prepared pans two-thirds full and bake for 18 to 20 minutes. Spoon glaze over tops and cool on a wire rack for 5 minutes. Remove muffins from pans and cool.

Glaze: Combine all ingredients and mix until sugar is dissolved.

*Two 9 x 5 x 3-inch loaf pans may be substituted for muffin pans. Bake at 350 degrees for 1 hour and cool on wire rack for 10 minutes before removing from pan.*

3 cups all-purpose flour
2 cups granulated sugar
1½ teaspoons baking powder
1½ teaspoons salt
3 eggs
1½ cups milk
½ cup butter
½ cup vegetable oil
1½ teaspoons vanilla extract
1½ teaspoons almond extract
3 tablespoons poppy seed
GLAZE:
¼ cup orange juice
¾ cup confectioners' sugar
½ teaspoon vanilla extract
½ teaspoon almond extract

**Never eat more than you can lift.**

*Miss Piggy*

SERVINGS
24 muffins

# Oatmeal Muffins

1½ cups packed brown sugar
1½ cups granulated sugar
1½ cups butter
2⅔ cups all-purpose flour
2¼ cups rolled oats
3 eggs, beaten
1½ cups buttermilk
1½ teaspoons baking soda
¾ teaspoon salt

Preheat oven to 375 degrees. Grease two 12-count muffin pans. In a large bowl combine sugars, butter, flour and oats. Reserve 1½ cups for topping. To remaining mixture add eggs, buttermilk, baking soda and salt. Beat until smooth. Fill prepared pans two-thirds full. Sprinkle muffins with reserved topping. Bake for 25 to 30 minutes. Cool on a wire rack for 5 minutes before removing from pans.

SERVINGS
12 muffins

# Broccoli Cheese Muffins

1 package (10 ounces) frozen chopped broccoli, thawed
½ cup diced onion
2 tablespoons butter
⅔ cup water
½ cup sour cream
1 egg
1 cup dry biscuit mix
1 cup (4 ounces) grated cheddar cheese

Preheat oven to 375 degrees. Grease a 12-count muffin pan. Drain broccoli and cut into small pieces. Sauté onion in butter until tender, 5 to 8 minutes. In a large bowl combine water, sour cream, egg and onion. Stir in biscuit mix. Fold in broccoli and cheese and spoon into muffin cups. Bake until golden brown, 35 to 40 minutes. Cool for 5 minutes before removing from pan. Serve warm.

SERVINGS
6 small loaves

# Great Pumpkin Bread

Preheat oven to 350 degrees. Grease six 5 x 3 x 2-inch loaf pans. Combine dry ingredients in a large bowl. Add remaining ingredients and mix well. Fill prepared pans half full and bake for 1 hour. Cool in pans on a wire rack.

**3½ cups all-purpose flour**
**1½ teaspoons salt**
**2 teaspoons baking soda**
**3 cups granulated sugar**
**1 teaspoon ground nutmeg**
**1 teaspoon ground cinnamon**
**1 can (16 ounces) solid pack pumpkin**
**1 cup vegetable oil**
**⅔ cup water**
**4 eggs**

SERVINGS
1 loaf

# Cranberry Nut Bread

Preheat oven to 325 degrees. Grease a 9 x 5 x 3-inch loaf pan. In a large bowl sift together flour, salt, baking powder, baking soda and sugar. In another bowl combine eggs, butter, water, orange juice, lemon juice and orange zest. Add egg mixture to dry ingredients and mix thoroughly. Fold in cranberries and pecans. Pour batter into prepared pan and bake for 1 hour. Remove from pan and cool on a wire rack.

**2 cups all-purpose flour**
**½ teaspoon salt**
**1½ teaspoons baking powder**
**½ teaspoon baking soda**
**1 cup granulated sugar**
**2 eggs, beaten**
**2 tablespoons butter, melted**
**2 tablespoons hot water**
**6 tablespoons orange juice**
**2 tablespoons lemon juice**
**1 tablespoon grated orange zest**
**1 cup fresh cranberries**
**½ cup chopped pecans**

SERVINGS
1 loaf

# FRESH APPLE BREAD

Preheat oven to 350 degrees. Grease and flour a 9 x 5 x 3-inch loaf pan. In a medium bowl sift together flour, baking soda, cinnamon and salt. Stir in pecans. Cream sugar and butter in a large bowl until fluffy. Stir in eggs and apple. Add flour mixture and mix well. Stir in buttermilk and vanilla. Pour into prepared pan. Combine sugar and cinnamon and sprinkle over batter. Bake until a wooden toothpick inserted in center comes out clean, about 1 hour. Cool for 10 minutes before removing from pan.

**2 cups all-purpose flour**
**1 teaspoon baking soda**
**1 teaspoon ground cinnamon**
**½ teaspoon salt**
**1 cup chopped pecans**
**1 cup granulated sugar**
**½ cup butter**
**2 eggs, beaten**
**1 cup grated apple**
**1½ tablespoons buttermilk**
**½ teaspoon vanilla extract**
**3 tablespoons granulated sugar**
**1 teaspoon ground cinnamon**

SERVINGS
2 loaves

# BOUNTIFUL ZUCCHINI BREAD

Preheat oven to 350 degrees. Grease and flour two 9 x 5 x 3-inch loaf pans. In a large bowl combine all ingredients and mix thoroughly. Divide batter and pour into prepared pans. Bake until a wooden toothpick inserted in center comes out clean, 1 to 1¼ hours. Cool for 10 minutes, remove from pans and cool on a wire rack.

**3 cups whole-wheat flour**
**2 cups granulated sugar**
**3 teaspoons ground cinnamon**
**1 teaspoon salt**
**1 teaspoon baking powder**
**1 teaspoon baking soda**
**3 teaspoons vanilla extract**
**1 cup vegetable oil**
**3 eggs**
**3 cups shredded zucchini**

SERVINGS
1 loaf

# CORN CORN BREAD

Preheat oven to 350 degrees. Grease a 9 x 5 x 3-inch loaf pan and dust with cornmeal. In a large bowl combine flour, cornmeal, sugar, baking powder, baking soda and salt. Whisk together eggs, oil, milk and buttermilk in a medium bowl. Add egg mixture to dry ingredients, stirring until just moistened. Fold corn into batter. Pour into prepared pan and bake for 15 minutes. Reduce heat to 325 degrees and continue baking until a wooden toothpick inserted in center comes out clean, about 1 hour. Cool on a wire rack for 30 minutes before removing from pan.

**1½ cups all-purpose flour**
**1¼ cups yellow cornmeal**
**¾ cup granulated sugar**
**½ teaspoon baking powder**
**½ teaspoon baking soda**
**½ teaspoon salt**

**2 large eggs**
**½ cup vegetable oil**
**½ cup milk**
**½ cup buttermilk**
**1 cup fresh corn, cooked**

**Bread is like dresses, hats and shoes–in other words, essential.**

*Emily Post*

SERVINGS
2 loaves

# PEASANT BREAD

Stir yeast, sugar and salt into water in a large bowl until dissolved. Let stand for 10 minutes. Stir in both flours but do not knead. Transfer dough into a large, greased bowl and turn to coat entire surface. Cover loosely with plastic wrap and a kitchen towel. Let rise in a warm, draft-free area until double in size, 1 to 1½ hours. Grease a baking sheet and dust with cornmeal. Divide and shape dough into two round or oblong loaves. Place loaves on baking sheet and let rise again until almost double, 35 to 45 minutes.

Preheat oven to 425 degrees. Brush tops of loaves with melted butter. Bake for 10 minutes then reduce heat to 375 degrees and bake for 20 minutes. Cool on a wire rack.

**1 package active dry yeast**
**2 tablespoon granulated sugar**
**1 teaspoon salt**
**2 cups warm water (110 to 115 degrees)**
**2 cups bread flour or all-purpose flour**
**2 cups whole-wheat or multi-grain flour**
**1 tablespoon cornmeal**
**1 tablespoon butter, melted**

SERVINGS
12-15

# GARLIC WEDGES

Preheat oven to 450 degrees. Place bread on baking sheet and brush with olive oil. In a small bowl combine mayonnaise, cheese, onion, basil and garlic. Spread over bread shell and bake until bubbly, 12 minutes. Cut into wedges. Serve warm.

**1 Italian bread shell (16 ounces)**
**1 tablespoon olive oil**
**½ cup mayonnaise**
**½ cup freshly grated Parmesan cheese**
**½ cup minced red onion**
**¼ cup minced fresh basil**
**3 or 4 large cloves garlic, minced**

SERVINGS
2 loaves

# LIBERTY LOAVES

2 cups water
1 cup rolled oats
½ cup honey
1 tablespoon butter
2 teaspoons salt
1 cup roasted sunflower kernels (optional)
1 package active dry yeast
½ cup warm water (110 to 115 degrees)
2½ cups whole-wheat flour
2 cups bread flour

Bring water to a boil and stir in oats. Set aside for 1 hour. Oil two 9 x 5 x 3-inch loaf pans and a large mixing bowl. Add honey, butter, salt and sunflower kernels to oat mixture and stir well. Dissolve yeast in warm water and allow to stand for 5 minutes. Stir softened yeast into oat mixture. Blend in flours until dough pulls cleanly away from sides of bowl. Form dough into ball and place in prepared bowl, turning to coat entire surface. Cover loosely with plastic wrap and a kitchen towel. Let rise in a warm draft-free area for 1 hour or until double in size. Punch down dough to remove air bubbles, then knead until smooth and elastic. Divide into two loaves and place in prepared pans. Cover and let rise again until double in size.

Preheat oven to 350 degrees. Bake until bread sounds hollow when tapped on bottom, 50 minutes. After baking for 35 minutes it may be necessary to shield loaves with foil to prevent over-browning. Remove bread from pans immediately and cool on a wire rack.

Bread that must be cut with an ax is bread that is too nourishing.

*Fran Lebowtiz*

SERVINGS
8

# Toasted Herb Bread

Preheat oven to 350 degrees. Cut bread in half lengthwise. Whisk together oil, garlic and fresh herbs (any combination of sage, thyme, oregano, rosemary, marjoram or basil). Brush bread with oil mixture and top with cheese and tomatoes or olives. Season with salt. Place on baking sheet and bake until lightly browned, 15 minutes. To serve, cut into 1-inch slices or wedges.

- 1 large loaf French bread or baked pizza crust
- ¼ cup olive oil
- 1 large clove garlic, minced
- 2 tablespoons fresh minced herbs
- ¼ cup freshly grated Parmesan cheese (optional)
- ¼ cup sliced kalamata olives or sun dried tomatoes (optional)
- ½ teaspoon kosher salt

SERVINGS
8

# Black Pepper & Onion Scones

Preheat oven to 400 degrees. Sauté onion in butter until crisp tender, 3 to 4 minutes. Set aside to cool slightly. In a medium bowl combine flour, sugar, baking powder, pepper and salt. Add cream, egg and onion. Stir until just moistened. On a floured surface knead dough 5 or 6 times. Place on a greased baking sheet and press into an 8-inch circle, ½ inch thick. Cut into 8 wedges, separate slightly and bake until lightly browned, 12 to 16 minutes. Brush with melted butter. Serve warm.

- ¾ cup diced onion
- ¼ cup butter
- 2 cups all-purpose flour
- 2 tablespoons granulated sugar
- 1 tablespoon baking powder
- ¾ teaspoon coarsely ground black pepper
- ½ teaspoon salt
- ½ cup heavy cream
- 1 egg
- 2 tablespoons butter, melted

SERVINGS
16 rolls

# ROLLED OAT ROLLS

2 to 2½ cups all-purpose flour, divided
⅓ cup rolled oats
¼ cup granulated sugar
1 teaspoon salt
1 package active dry yeast
1 cup milk
3 tablespoons butter
1 egg, room temperature
¾ cup whole-wheat flour
1 egg white
1 tablespoon water
1 tablespoon rolled oats

Combine 1 cup flour, rolled oats, sugar, salt and yeast in a large bowl. In a small saucepan heat milk and butter to 120 to 130 degrees. Add milk mixture and egg to dry ingredients. Blend with electric mixer at low speed until moistened. Beat for 2 minutes at medium speed. Add whole-wheat flour and an additional ¾ to 1 cup all-purpose flour. Stir until dough pulls cleanly away from sides of bowl. Turn onto a lightly floured surface. Knead in ¼ to ¾ cup all-purpose flour until dough is smooth and elastic, about 5 minutes. Form into a ball and place in a greased bowl, turning to coat entire surface. Cover loosely with plastic wrap and a kitchen towel. Let rise in a warm, draft-free area until double in size, about 1 hour.

Grease a 9-inch square pan. Punch down dough to remove air bubbles. Divide dough into 16 pieces and shape into balls. Place in prepared pan and cover loosely with plastic wrap and a kitchen towel. Let rise in a warm place until double in size, 35 to 45 minutes.

Preheat oven to 375 degrees. Beat egg white and water in a small bowl, brush glaze over rolls and sprinkle with 1 tablespoon rolled oats. Bake until golden brown, 20 to 25 minutes. Remove from pan and serve warm.

**If at first you don't succeed, try reading the directions.**

*unknown*

SERVINGS
36 rolls

# Freedom Rolls

2 cups whole milk
½ cup granulated sugar
½ cup butter
1 package active dry yeast
¾ teaspoon baking powder
½ teaspoon baking soda
½ teaspoon salt
4 cups all-purpose flour
Melted butter, for baking

Bring milk, sugar and butter to a boil, remove from heat and cool until lukewarm (110 to 115 degrees). Stir in yeast, baking powder, baking soda and salt.

Combine flour and milk mixture in a large bowl, stirring until dough pulls cleanly away from sides. (Add up to an additional ½ cup of flour if necessary.) Lightly oil top of dough and cover with plastic wrap and a kitchen towel. Set in a warm, draft-free area until double in size, about 2 hours.

Punch down dough and fold edges to center. Turn dough over and brush with oil. Place in a plastic container with a tight-fitting lid and chill for at least 6 hours or up to 1 week. Punch down dough if it rises in refrigerator.

Lightly oil a baking sheet. Roll 2 tablespoons dough into a 6-inch length. Loop around to form a knot. Place on prepared baking sheet. Repeat with remaining dough. Brush tops lightly with melted butter and cover with plastic wrap and a kitchen towel. Allow to rise until double in size, about 2 hours.

Preheat oven to 400 degrees. Bake rolls until light golden brown, 8 to 10 minutes. Remove from oven and brush lightly with melted butter.

*This basic dough may be used for crescent, cloverleaf and Parkerhouse rolls or with a favorite sweet roll filling.*

SERVINGS
36 rolls

# TINY CINNS

Combine yeast, sugar and sour cream. Let stand for 10 minutes. Place flour, butter, sugar and salt in food processor and pulse 3 or 4 times. Add egg yolks and yeast mixture. Pulse only until combined. Do not overprocess. Cover and chill several hours or overnight.

Grease three 12-count mini-muffin pans. In a saucepan combine brown sugar and water and bring to a boil. Add butter and stir until melted. Spoon 1 teaspoon mixture into each muffin cup. Place a pecan half, upside down, in each cup.

Combine brown sugar, cinnamon, raisins and pecans in a small bowl.

Divide dough into four parts. On a heavily floured board, roll dough into a 9 x 3-inch rectangle. Brush with 1 tablespoon butter and sprinkle with one-fourth of the cinnamon mixture. Lightly press into dough with rolling pin. From 9-inch side, roll up dough, pinching seam and ends to seal. Cut into 9 slices. Place slices in muffin pans and press down lightly. Brush tops with butter. Repeat with remaining dough. Cover loosely with plastic wrap and a kitchen towel. Let rise in warm, draft-free area until double in size.

Preheat oven to 375 degrees. Place muffin pans on upper rack and bake for 15 to 20 minutes. Invert pans immediately.

1 package active dry yeast
1 teaspoon granulated sugar
1 cup sour cream, warmed to 110 degrees.
2 cups all-purpose flour
½ cup butter, cut into 6 pieces
1 tablespoon granulated sugar
1 teaspoon salt
3 large egg yolks
⅓ cup packed light brown sugar
¼ cup hot water
5 tablespoons butter
36 pecan halves
¼ cup packed dark brown sugar
1 teaspoon ground cinnamon
½ cup golden raisins
1 cup chopped pecans
6 tablespoons butter, melted

We don't call it sin today, we call it self-expression.

*Baroness Stocks*

JOAN OF ARC

# SAINTLY ENTRÉES

## How a simple French girl became a flaming success.

In the fifteenth century, France was in a food funk. The people's palates were jaded — tired of truffles, sick of soufflés, bored with béchamel. If this trend continued, the very soul of France would be lost. ❖ Then, a teenage scullery maid in the village of Orléans heard a voice bubbling out of a pot of bouillabaisse. ❖ "Pssst! Joan!" said the voice. "Only you have the power to inflame the tuckered tastebuds of France." ❖ So with determination befitting a holy mission, Joan set out to make eating fun again for all the French people. ❖ First she tried decorating plates with vegetables formed into risqué shapes. The people yawned. Then Joan resorted to meats chopped and formed into perfect models of famous architectural landmarks. The people's verdict was: interesting but not appetizing. ❖ Finally, in a fit of petty pique, Joan of Arc put the torch to a plateful of *boeuf* with cognac and Roquefort sauce. The diners were amazed, and suddenly, inexplicably hungry. The craze for flambé spread across France like...well, like wildfire. ❖ Joan became a national heroine. Her feats with flame grew larger and more impressive. Until, at the height of her popularity, she attempted to flambé a world-record apple tart. ❖ POOF! Joan sizzled her way to sainthood. ❖ You, however, don't need flames to create a saintly entrée. The following entrées will light up any table.

Entrées

SERVINGS
4

# SEARED FILLETS WITH SHIITAKE LEEK SAUCE

4 tenderloin fillets, 6 ounces each
Salt and freshly ground pepper, to taste
1 tablespoon olive oil
1 large leek, sliced (white and light green part only)
½ pound fresh shiitake mushroom caps, sliced
½ teaspoon salt
½ cup beef broth
½ cup dry red wine
1 tablespoon snipped fresh chives

Preheat oven to 425 degrees. Season beef with salt and pepper. In an ovenproof sauté pan sear beef in hot oil for 1 to 2 minutes per side. Remove from pan and set aside. In same pan sauté leek and mushrooms until liquid evaporates. Add salt, beef broth and wine. Bring to a boil and return meat to pan. Place pan in oven until fillets reach an internal temperature of 135 degrees for medium-rare, 10 to 15 minutes. Remove fillets to serving plate. Cook sauce over high heat until thickened, stirring constantly. Add chives to sauce and spoon over fillets.

SERVINGS
8-10

# ROASTED TENDERLOIN

4 to 6 pounds beef tenderloin
2 teaspoons ground thyme
½ teaspoon white pepper
1 teaspoon garlic salt
¼ teaspoon dried oregano
1 tablespoon seasoned salt
¼ cup Worcestershire sauce

Place tenderloin on a large piece of foil and rub with thyme. Combine white pepper, garlic salt, oregano and seasoned salt. Thoroughly coat beef with seasonings. Seal foil and chill for 12 hours.

Remove tenderloin from refrigerator 1 hour before roasting. Preheat oven to 400 degrees. Pour 1 cup water in bottom of broiler pan. Remove foil and place tenderloin on rack. Sprinkle meat with Worcestershire sauce. Roast to an internal temperature of 130 degrees for medium-rare, 40 minutes. Remove from oven and let stand for 10 minutes before slicing.

SERVINGS
4

# Cold Peppered Tenderloin with Tarragon Sauce

Preheat oven to 500 degrees. Pat tenderloin dry and rub all sides with salt and pepper. In a roasting pan just large enough to hold tenderloin, brown meat on all sides in hot oil. Place in oven and roast for 15 to 20 minutes or to an internal temperature of 130 degrees for medium-rare. Cool to room temperature. (Tenderloin may be roasted 2 days in advance, wrapped in foil and chilled.) Carve tenderloin in thin slices. Arrange on a serving platter and top with chilled sauce. Serve remaining sauce on the side.

Tarragon Sauce: Blend cream, vinegar, Worcestershire sauce and mustard in a food processor. With processor running, add oil in a steady stream to form a thin sauce. Transfer mixture to a small bowl and stir in tarragon, capers, onions, parsley and salt. Cover and chill. Sauce may be made 1 day ahead.

1½ to 2 pounds beef tenderloin, room temperature
1 tablespoon coarsely ground black pepper
1 teaspoon coarse kosher salt
1 tablespoon vegetable oil
TARRAGON SAUCE:
2 tablespoons heavy cream
2 tablespoons white wine vinegar
1 teaspoon Worcestershire sauce
1½ teaspoons Dijon mustard
½ cup olive oil
1½ teaspoons minced fresh tarragon
1 tablespoon capers, drained
2 tablespoons thinly sliced green onions
2 tablespoons minced fresh parsley
Salt, to taste

**Roast beef, medium, is not only a food. It is a philosophy.**

*Edna Ferber*

SERVINGS
8

# BRAISED BEEF IN GREEN PEPPERCORN SAUCE

In a Dutch oven brown meat on all sides in hot oil. Season generously with salt and pepper. Add water, cover and simmer until meat is tender, 2½ to 3 hours. Remove from pan and let stand for 20 minutes then slice thin.

Preheat oven to 350 degrees. Spoon half of sauce over bottom of a shallow ovenproof serving platter. Arrange meat slices in sauce, slightly overlapping. Pour remaining sauce over top. (May be prepared ahead to this point.) Just before serving bake until thoroughly heated, 10 minutes. Spoon sauce over meat and sprinkle generously with parsley.

Sauce: Heat butter in a medium saucepan until it bubbles and browns. Whisk in cream, garlic, lemon juice, mustard, salt and peppercorns. Stir over medium heat for about 3 minutes, reducing sauce slightly.

**4 pounds boneless roast (sirloin tip, bottom round or rump roast)**
**2 tablespoons vegetable oil**
**Salt and freshly ground pepper, to taste**
**½ cup water**
**GREEN PEPPERCORN SAUCE:**
**¼ cup butter**
**2 cups heavy cream**
**2 large cloves garlic, minced**
**2 tablespoons fresh lemon juice**
**2 teaspoons Dijon mustard**
**1½ teaspoons salt**
**2 teaspoons green peppercorns packed in water**
**½ cup minced fresh parsley**

SERVINGS
4

# JOAN'S KABOBS

Whisk marinade ingredients until well blended. Marinate sirloin for 2 to 3 hours. Alternate sirloin and vegetables on skewers. Grill over medium coals for 3 to 4 minutes per side. Baste kabobs during grilling.

**1½ pounds sirloin, cut into 1-inch cubes**
**2 red bell peppers, cut into 1-inch pieces**
**8 fresh mushrooms**
**8 fresh pearl onions**
**MARINADE:**
**⅓ cup barbecue sauce**
**½ cup soy sauce**
**¼ cup vegetable oil**
**¼ cup white wine**
**2 cloves garlic, minced**
**½ teaspoon MSG (optional)**

SERVINGS
6-8

# Grilled Peppered Steaks

Whisk oil, vinegar, mustard, garlic, shallots, pepper, thyme, rosemary and salt until well blended. Place steaks in single layer in a large baking dish. Pour marinade over meat and turn to coat. Cover and chill overnight.

Remove steaks from marinade and season both sides generously with pepper. Grill steaks over medium coals, about 4 minutes per side for medium-rare. Carve steaks diagonally into thin slices across grain. Arrange slices on platter and garnish with rosemary.

**¾ cup olive oil**
**⅓ cup red wine vinegar**
**4½ tablespoons Dijon mustard**
**4 large cloves garlic, minced**
**2 large shallots, minced**
**1 tablespoon coarsely ground black pepper**
**1 tablespoon minced fresh thyme, or 1 teaspoon dried**
**1 tablespoon minced fresh rosemary, or 1 teaspoon dried**
**1 teaspoon salt**
**2 flank steaks (1¼ pounds each)**
**Freshly ground pepper, to taste**
**Rosemary sprigs for garnish**

SERVINGS
4-6

# Three Bean Casserole

Preheat oven to 350 degrees. Grease a 4-quart casserole dish. Cook bacon until crisp and drain, reserving 2 tablespoons drippings. Crumble bacon and set aside. Sauté onions in reserved drippings until tender. Drain and set aside. Brown ground beef, stirring to remove lumps and drain. Combine all ingredients and pour into prepared casserole dish. Bake covered for 1 hour.

**½ pound bacon**
**1 medium onion, diced**
**1½ pounds lean ground beef**
**1 can (15 ounces) red kidney beans, drained**
**1 can (15 ounces) pork and beans**
**1 can (15 ounces) butter beans, drained**
**¼ cup packed brown sugar**
**¼ cup granulated sugar**
**½ teaspoon chili powder**
**¼ cup barbecue sauce**
**¼ cup ketchup**
**2 tablespoons prepared mustard**
**2 tablespoons molasses**
**1 teaspoon salt**
**½ teaspoon black pepper**

SERVINGS
12

# ÉNCREDIBLE ENCHILADAS

Shredded Beef: Place ingredients in a Dutch oven and bring to a boil. Reduce heat and simmer for 3 hours. Drain and discard onion. Cool then shred beef.

Sauce: Combine ingredients in a saucepan and simmer for 30 minutes.

Filling: Sauté onion and jalapeño peppers in oil until tender. Add tomatoes, olives, chili powder, cumin, salt and pepper. Stir in shredded beef and ½ cup sauce.

Preheat oven to 350 degrees. Soften tortillas in microwave for 10 seconds. Pour ½ cup sauce in bottom of 14 x 10-inch baking dish. Place ⅓ cup filling and ¼ cup grated cheese on each tortilla. Roll up and place seam side down in pan. Combine remaining sauce, tomatoes and green chilies and pour over casserole. Top with remaining cheese. Bake for 20 to 25 minutes. Serve with green onions and sour cream on the side.

**SHREDDED BEEF:**
2 pound eye of round roast
1 onion, cut into quarters
4 cups beef broth
3 tablespoons vinegar
1 tablespoon chili powder
1 tablespoon ground cumin

**SAUCE:**
2½ cups tomato sauce
2 tablespoons vegetable oil
1 tablespoon ground cumin
¾ teaspoon chili powder
½ teaspoon salt
¼ teaspoon black pepper
⅛ teaspoon hot pepper sauce

**FILLING:**
1 medium onion, diced
6 to 8 fresh jalapeño peppers, seeded and diced
2 tablespoons vegetable oil
1 can (14½ ounces) diced tomatoes, drained
¾ cup sliced black olives
1 teaspoon chili powder
1 teaspoon ground cumin
1 teaspoon salt
½ teaspoon black pepper
12 flour tortillas (10-inch), heated in microwave to soften
8 cups (32 ounces) grated Monterey Jack cheese
1 can (14½ ounces) diced tomatoes, drained
1 can (4½ ounces) chopped green chilies
1 bunch green onions, thinly sliced
Sour cream for topping

SERVINGS 8

# TAILGATERS' CHILI PIE

Preheat oven to 350 degrees. In a 3-quart casserole dish combine beef, beans and green chilies. Combine onion soup mix, tomato sauce, beer, water and chili powder. Add to beef mixture. Bake covered until beef is tender, 1½ hours. Combine corn bread mix with egg and milk. Stir in cheese and spread evenly over casserole. Bake uncovered until golden, 25 minutes.

*Wrap hot casserole tightly in foil and place in an ice chest for a tailgate party or picnic.*

**2 pounds boneless chuck steak, cut into ½-inch cubes**
**1 can (15½ ounces) kidney beans, with liquid**
**1 can (4½ ounces) chopped green chilies**
**1 envelope (1 ounce) dry onion soup mix**
**1 can (8 ounces) tomato sauce**
**1 can (12 ounces) beer**
**¼ cup water**
**1½ tablespoons chili powder**
**1 package (8½ ounces) corn bread mix**
**1 egg**
**⅓ cup milk**
**1 cup (4 ounces) grated cheddar cheese**

Gourmets dig their graves with their teeth.

*French Proverb*

SERVINGS
1½ cups

# Beef Baron Marinade

Whisk all ingredients except oil. Slowly add oil and continue to whisk until well blended. Marinate desired cut of beef for 2 to 12 hours. Use remaining marinade for basting during cooking.

- 1 cup dry red wine
- 3 tablespoons Worcestershire sauce
- 2 teaspoons salt
- 2 teaspoons black pepper
- 2 tablespoons fresh lemon juice
- 1 clove garlic, minced
- 2 tablespoons dried minced onion
- ¼ cup vegetable oil

SERVINGS
1½ cups

# Teriyaki Marinade

Mix together all ingredients. Pour over chicken, pork or beef. Cover and chill for at least 3 hours or overnight. Meat may be grilled or broiled.

- ½ cup soy sauce
- ½ cup dry white wine
- 2 tablespoons granulated sugar
- ¼ cup packed brown sugar
- 1 teaspoon finely grated ginger root or ¼ teaspoon ground ginger
- 1 or 2 cloves garlic, minced
- 1 teaspoon vegetable oil

SERVINGS
4

# VEAL CHOPS WITH PINE NUT SAUCE

Season veal with salt and pepper. Cook bacon until crisp. Drain, crumble and set aside. Add oil to skillet and brown veal 3 to 5 minutes per side. Remove from skillet and keep warm. Pour sauce over veal and sprinkle with crumbled bacon.

Pine Nut Sauce: Sauté shallot and garlic in oil for 2 minutes. Add tomatoes, pine nuts, capers, basil, herbes, wine and lemon juice and cook for 2 minutes. Stir in butter.

*Turkey breast medallions may be substituted for veal.*

4 veal chops, boned and trimmed
Salt and freshly ground pepper, to taste
3 slices bacon
1 tablespoon olive oil
PINE NUT SAUCE:
1 shallot, minced
2 cloves garlic, minced
1 tablespoon olive oil
4 plum tomatoes, diced
⅓ cup pine nuts, toasted
2 tablespoons capers
1 teaspoon dried basil
1 teaspoon dried fines herbes
1 tablespoon white wine
1 tablespoon lemon juice
2 tablespoons butter

SERVINGS
2

# VEAL À LA NORMANDE

Cut veal into serving pieces and pound thin. Sauté apples in butter until they begin to brown. Remove with a slotted spoon and set aside. Season veal with salt and pepper and brown until done, about 3 minutes per side. Add more butter if necessary. Remove veal to serving plates. Remove pan from heat, add Calvados and stir to deglaze pan. Return pan to heat, stir in cream and apples and heat through. Spoon apples over veal and serve immediately.

½ pound veal round
2 Granny Smith apples, peeled and thinly sliced
2 tablespoons butter
Salt and freshly ground pepper, to taste
¼ cup Calvados brandy
¼ cup heavy cream

SERVINGS
4

# Veal Chops with Artichoke Sauce

Preheat oven to 400 degrees. Boil chicken broth until reduced to 1 cup. In a skillet large enough to hold all 4 veal chops, melt ¼ cup butter. Sauté mushrooms until tender, about 8 minutes. Remove and set aside. Add oil and brown chops on both sides. Transfer chops to baking dish and place in oven for 10 minutes for medium-rare. While chops are baking, pour wine in skillet and deglaze pan. Add broth, remaining butter, artichokes, tomatoes, mushrooms and herbs. Stir until thoroughly heated. Spoon sauce over chops before serving.

**3 cups chicken broth**
**½ cup butter, divided**
**1 pound fresh mushrooms, sliced**
**2 tablespoons olive oil**
**4 veal chops**
**½ cup Madeira wine**
**¾ cup sliced artichoke bottoms**
**2 tomatoes, peeled, seeded and diced**
**1 tablespoon fresh minced parsley**
**1 tablespoon fresh snipped chives**
**½ teaspoon dried thyme**

SERVINGS
6

# Orange Mustard Lamb Kabobs

Combine marmalade, orange juice, mustard, allspice and salt. Pour over lamb, cover and chill for 2 hours. Thread lamb onto skewers and grill over medium coals for 10 to 15 minutes, turning frequently. Baste with marinade during grilling. Serve with Vermicelli Pilaf (page 184).

**1 cup orange marmalade**
**½ cup fresh orange juice**
**¼ cup Dijon mustard**
**2 teaspoons ground allspice**
**½ teaspoon salt**
**2 pounds lamb (leg or shoulder), cut into 1½-inch cubes**

SERVINGS 4

# LAMB CHOPS WITH MINT PESTO

Place lamb chops in a large baking dish and season with garlic, salt, pepper, mint and olive oil. Cover and chill for at least 6 hours. Grill chops over medium coals. Turn occasionally until well browned, 3 to 4 minutes per side for medium-rare. Serve lamb chops with pesto on the side.

Mint Pesto: Blend all ingredients in a food processor until a coarse paste forms.

8 lamb rib chops
2 cloves garlic, minced
½ teaspoon salt
½ teaspoon freshly ground pepper
2 tablespoons minced fresh mint or 2 teaspoons dried mint
2 tablespoons olive oil

MINT PESTO:
2 cups loosely packed fresh mint leaves
½ cup loosely packed parsley leaves
2 cloves garlic, peeled
¼ cup extra virgin oil
¼ teaspoon salt
⅛ teaspoon freshly ground pepper
½ cup freshly grated Parmesan cheese
¼ cup pine nuts or walnuts, toasted
1 tablespoon fresh lemon juice

People who fight fire with fire usually end up with ashes.

*Abigail Van Buren*

SERVINGS
8-10

# Glazed Lamb Roast

Leg of lamb, boned and rolled (4 to 5 pounds)
1 jar (12 ounces) chili sauce
1 jar (10 ounces) currant jelly
¼ cup mint sauce with leaves

Preheat oven to 475 degrees. Roast lamb for 30 minutes. While lamb is cooking, warm remaining ingredients in a small saucepan. Reduce heat to 325 degrees and baste lamb with sauce. Roast for 20 minutes per pound, basting occasionally. Remove from oven and let stand for 10 minutes before carving. Warm remaining sauce and serve on the side.

SERVINGS
6

# Pork Tenderloin with Sautéed Apples

2 tablespoons balsamic vinegar
2 tablespoons coriander seed, cracked
1 tablespoon soy sauce
1 tablespoon black peppercorns, freshly cracked
3 cloves garlic, minced
2 teaspoons olive oil
5 or 6 sprigs fresh marjoram, minced
2 pork tenderloins, trimmed
1½ teaspoons vegetable oil
Salt and freshly ground pepper, to taste
4 apples, cut into eighths (McIntosh or Granny Smith)
1½ teaspoons butter
1 cup apple cider
Marjoram sprigs for garnish

Combine vinegar, coriander, soy sauce, peppercorns, garlic, olive oil and marjoram in a small bowl. Place pork in a 13 x 9-inch nonmetallic baking dish. Spread marinade over pork, cover and chill for 2 to 4 hours, turning several times. Let stand at room temperature for 20 minutes before cooking.

Preheat oven to 425 degrees. In a large skillet brown pork in oil, about 2 minutes per side. Place pork in a lightly oiled roasting pan and cover with remaining marinade. Roast to an internal temperature of 160 degrees for medium well, 10 to 15 minutes.

Sauté apples in butter until they begin to turn golden, 3 to 5 minutes. Sprinkle with salt and pepper, add cider and simmer until apples are tender, about 4 minutes. Carve pork into thick slices and arrange on serving plates. Spoon apples with liquid over pork. Garnish with marjoram.

SERVINGS
12

# Crown Roast of Pork with Fennel Stuffing

2 teaspoons salt
1 teaspoon freshly ground pepper
1½ teaspoons dried thyme
1½ teaspoons rubbed sage
16 rib crown roast of pork (about 8 pounds)
Vegetable oil
Fresh fennel fronds for garnish

FENNEL STUFFING:
1½ cups wild rice
2 teaspoons fennel seed
3 cups chicken broth
1½ cups water
1 pound sweet Italian sausage, casings removed
2 cups diced onion
¼ cup unsalted butter
3 small fennel bulbs, diced (about 3 cups)
Salt and freshly ground pepper, to taste

In a small bowl combine salt, pepper, thyme and sage. Rub mixture over the roast, cover and chill overnight.

Preheat oven to 450 degrees. Lightly oil a roasting pan. Pat roast dry with paper towels and rub with vegetable oil. Cut two pieces of heavy-duty foil slightly larger than bottom of roast and lightly oil. Place one in center of roasting pan. Place roast on foil and mound stuffing into center of crown. Cover stuffing with remaining round of foil. Roast for 20 minutes, reduce heat to 325 degrees and roast for 1¾ hours or to an internal temperature of 160 degrees for medium-well. (Roast for 2 hours or to 170 degrees for well-done). Transfer roast with foil underneath to a serving platter and let stand for 15 minutes. Remove foil and discard. Garnish with fennel fronds and cover rib tips with papillotes.

Fennel Stuffing: Combine rice, fennel seed, chicken broth and water in a Dutch oven. Bring to a boil, reduce heat and simmer partially covered until rice is tender, 45 to 55 minutes. Drain. In a heavy skillet over medium heat, cook sausage until it is no longer pink, stirring to break up lumps. Drain well and add to rice mixture. Sauté onion in butter until tender. Add fennel and cook covered, stirring occasionally until fennel is crisp tender, 5 to 7 minutes. Combine with sausage mixture, and season to taste. Cool slightly, cover and chill for up to 2 days. Bring to room temperature before stuffing roast.

SERVINGS
4-6

# Pork Tenderloin with Mustard Tarragon Sauce

Trim fat from tenderloins. Season generously with garlic salt and pepper. Grill over medium coals for 4 to 5 minutes per side (total of 16 to 20 minutes for all 4 sides) or to an internal temperature of 160 degrees. Remove from grill and let stand for 5 minutes before slicing. Cut into ¾-inch slices. Arrange on a platter and top with sauce. Serve remaining sauce on the side.

Mustard Tarragon Sauce: Mix butter and mustard in a small bowl and set aside. Combine onion, wine and tarragon in a small saucepan. Bring to a boil and cook over medium heat until wine is reduced to about ½ cup. Whisk in butter and mustard a small amount at a time. Stir in cream, salt and pepper.

**2 or 3 pork tenderloins**
**Garlic salt and freshly ground pepper, to taste**
**MUSTARD TARRAGON SAUCE:**
**6 tablespoons butter, softened**
**¼ cup Dijon mustard**
**½ cup finely minced onion or shallots**
**2 cups dry white wine**
**3 tablespoons minced fresh tarragon**
**2 to 4 tablespoons heavy cream**
**Salt and freshly ground pepper, to taste**

SERVINGS
6

# Glazed Spareribs

Preheat oven to 450 degrees. Arrange ribs in a large shallow pan. Bake for 20 minutes. Remove from oven and drain pan drippings. Reduce heat to 350 degrees. Combine jam and mustard and spread over top of ribs. Bake for 1 hour.

**5 to 6 pounds spareribs or country style boneless ribs**
**1 cup apricot or peach jam**
**3 tablespoons prepared mustard**

SERVINGS
8-10

# HERBED PORK ROAST WITH MUSHROOMS

5 tablespoons olive oil, divided
3 or 4 cloves garlic, minced
1 teaspoon dried rosemary
1 teaspoon dried thyme
1 teaspoon salt
1 teaspoon peppercorns, freshly cracked
¼ teaspoon ground allspice
4 pounds boneless pork loin, tied
SHERRY MUSHROOM SAUCE:
1 pound fresh mushrooms, sliced
¼ cup butter
½ cup dry sherry
1½ tablespoons water
1 tablespoon cornstarch

Combine 4 tablespoons oil, garlic, rosemary, thyme, salt, peppercorns and allspice in a small bowl. Rub into roast. Cover and chill for several hours or overnight.

Preheat oven to 350 degrees. Brown pork in 1 tablespoon olive oil in roasting pan, 2 minutes per side. Roast in oven until meat reaches an internal temperature of 160 degrees and juices run clear, 60 to 70 minutes. Let stand for 10 minutes before slicing. Serve with sauce.

Sherry Mushroom Sauce: During last 30 minutes of cooking, prepare mushroom sauce. Sauté mushrooms in butter over medium heat about 5 minutes. Add sherry and simmer for 20 to 25 minutes. Whisk water and cornstarch until smooth and gradually add to mushrooms, stirring until sauce thickens.

There were two subjects of conversation; one was the food they were eating and the other was the food they had eaten at other times.

*Unknown*

SERVINGS
4

# Sausage & Ham Jambalaya

Brown sausage over medium heat. Remove with a slotted spoon and drain on paper towels. Add onion, bell pepper and garlic clove to drippings. Sauté until tender, about 5 minutes. Stir in sausage, ham, wine, tomatoes with liquid, thyme, basil, marjoram, paprika and hot pepper sauce. Bring mixture to a boil and stir in rice. Reduce heat, cover and simmer until rice is just done, 20 to 25 minutes. Sprinkle with parsley.

**2 cups smoked sausage, sliced**
**1 cup diced yellow onion**
**¾ cup diced green bell pepper**
**1 large clove garlic, peeled**
**2 cups diced ham**
**½ cup dry white wine**
**1 can (14½ ounces) tomatoes, with liquid**
**½ teaspoon dried thyme**
**¼ teaspoon dried basil**
**¼ teaspoon dried marjoram**
**¼ teaspoon paprika**
**¼ teaspoon hot pepper sauce**
**¾ cup long-grain white rice**
**2 tablespoons minced fresh parsley**

SERVINGS
6

# Bon Temps Red Beans & Rice

Soak beans at least 10 hours or overnight. Drain. In a Dutch oven combine beans, water, ham, bay leaves, sugar, salt, cumin, hot pepper sauce and red pepper. Bring to a boil, reduce heat and simmer, stirring occasionally. Brown sausage, onion and garlic in a skillet. Drain well and add to beans. Bring mixture to boil, reduce heat and simmer partially covered until beans are very tender, 3 hours. Stir occasionally and add water as necessary. When beans are cooked, discard bay leaves. Remove 2 cups of beans and mash. Return mashed beans to pan, stir and simmer for 10 minutes. Serve in bowls with a scoop of rice in center.

**16 ounces small red beans**
**8 cups water**
**½ pound smoked ham, diced**
**2 bay leaves**
**1 tablespoon granulated sugar**
**1 teaspoon salt**
**½ teaspoon ground cumin**
**¼ teaspoon hot pepper sauce, or more to taste**
**⅛ teaspoon ground red pepper, or more to taste**
**1 pound andouille sausage, casings removed and sliced**
**½ pound Polish sausage, sliced**
**1 large onion, diced**
**3 cloves garlic, minced**
**Rice**

SERVINGS
4

# IMPERIAL CHICKEN WITH MADEIRA MUSHROOMS

Preheat oven to 350 degrees. Grease a 9x9-inch baking dish. In a small bowl combine cheese, bread crumbs, parsley, salt, pepper and garlic powder. Dip chicken in butter and coat with crumb mixture. Roll up and secure with a toothpick. Place seam side down in prepared baking dish. Moisten top of chicken with lemon juice and sprinkle with paprika. Bake for 45 minutes. When chicken becomes golden, cover loosely with foil to prevent overbrowning. Remove toothpicks and spoon sauce over chicken.

Madeira Sauce: Sauté shallots in butter over medium low heat until tender. Increase heat to medium high, add mushrooms and sauté for 3 to 5 minutes. Add wine and boil until liquid completely evaporates. Sprinkle mushrooms with flour and cook for 1 minute. Stir in chicken broth and cream. Boil until sauce thickens, stirring constantly. Add parsley, nutmeg, salt and pepper.

**1/3 cup freshly grated Parmesan cheese**
**1/2 cup dry bread crumbs**
**2 tablespoons minced fresh parsley**
**Salt and freshly ground pepper, to taste**
**1/2 teaspoon garlic powder**
**4 chicken breast halves, skinned and boned**
**1/2 cup butter, melted**
**Juice of 1/2 lemon**
**Paprika**
**MADEIRA SAUCE:**
**2 shallots, minced**
**2 tablespoons butter**
**4 ounces fresh mushrooms, sliced**
**1/4 cup Madeira wine**
**1 teaspoon all-purpose flour**
**1/2 cup chicken broth**
**1 cup heavy cream**
**2 tablespoons minced fresh parsley**
**1/8 teaspoon ground nutmeg**
**1/2 teaspoon salt**
**Freshly ground pepper, to taste**

SERVINGS
4-6

# Garlic Roasted Chicken

1 chicken (3 to 4 pounds)
4 cloves garlic, minced
½ cup minced fresh herbs (any combination of thyme, sage, rosemary, marjoram, tarragon or basil)
½ teaspoon salt
¼ teaspoon black pepper
2 tablespoons olive oil

Soak chicken in salted water for 10 minutes. Mash together garlic, herbs, salt and pepper. Add olive oil to form a paste. Remove chicken from water and pat dry. Loosen skin around chicken. Divide herb mixture and push under skin, covering as much of the chicken as possible. (At this point, chicken may be covered and chilled for up to 24 hours.)

Preheat oven to 450 degrees. Lightly oil chicken. Place chicken, breast side up, in pan and roast for 15 minutes. Reduce heat to 350 degrees and turn chicken on its side. Baste with drippings and roast for 15 minutes. Turn chicken to other side, baste and roast for 15 minutes. Turn chicken breast side down, baste and roast for 15 minutes. Turn chicken breast side up, and roast for another 15 to 30 minutes, basting frequently until it reaches an internal temperature of 165 degrees. Remove from oven and let stand for 15 minutes before carving.

SERVINGS
8

# STUFFED CHICKEN BREASTS WITH CILANTRO DRESSING

Preheat oven to 425 degrees. Combine cheese, onions, cilantro, garlic and cumin in a medium bowl. Loosen skin from each piece of chicken and fill with ¼ cup dressing. Arrange stuffed breasts, skin side up, in a single layer in broiler pan or shallow roasting pan. Sprinkle chicken with oil, salt and pepper. Bake until skin is golden and juices run clear when chicken is pierced with a fork, 25 to 30 minutes. Serve chicken hot, topped with chilled dressing.

Cilantro Dressing: Combine cilantro, sour cream, mayonnaise, lime juice and garlic in food processor until smooth. Stir in lime zest, salt and pepper. Cover and chill.

**1½ cups (6 ounces) grated Monterey Jack cheese**
**3 tablespoons thinly sliced green onions**
**4 teaspoons minced fresh cilantro**
**1 clove garlic, minced**
**¾ teaspoon ground cumin**
**8 chicken breast halves, with skin, boned**
**¼ cup olive oil**
**Salt and freshly ground pepper, to taste**
**CILANTRO DRESSING:**
**1 cup minced fresh cilantro leaves, lightly packed**
**1 cup light sour cream**
**½ cup light mayonnaise**
**2 tablespoons fresh lime juice**
**½ teaspoon minced garlic**
**¼ teaspoon grated lime zest**
**¼ teaspoon salt**
**⅛ teaspoon black pepper**

**Send me out into another life . . .**
**But get me back for supper.**

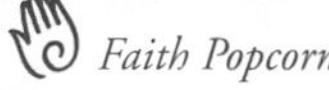

*Faith Popcorn*

SERVINGS
8

# Crab Stuffed Chicken Breasts

- ¼ pound fresh mushrooms, sliced
- ½ cup green onions, thinly sliced
- ¼ cup butter
- 3 tablespoons all-purpose flour
- ¼ teaspoon dried thyme
- ½ cup chicken broth
- ½ cup milk
- ½ cup dry white wine
- 8 ounces crabmeat, flaked
- ⅓ cup minced fresh parsley
- ⅓ cup dry bread crumbs
- 8 chicken breast halves, skinned, boned and pounded thin
- 1½ cups (6 ounces) grated Swiss cheese

Sauté mushrooms and onions in butter until tender. Stir in flour and thyme, cooking until bubbly. Gradually stir in chicken broth, milk and wine. Cook until sauce thickens.

Grease a 13 x 9-inch casserole dish. Combine ¼ cup sauce with crabmeat, parsley and bread crumbs in a medium bowl. Spread equal amounts over each chicken breast. Roll up and place seam side down in prepared dish. Pour remaining sauce over chicken and sprinkle with cheese. Cover and chill for up to 24 hours.

Preheat oven to 400 degrees and bake covered for 30 to 35 minutes. Uncover and bake until lightly browned, 5 minutes.

**Some people pretend to like capers, but the truth is that any dish that tastes good with capers in it tastes even better with capers not in it.**

*Nora Ephron*

SERVINGS
2

# BAKED CHICKEN WITH BLACK BEAN SAUCE

Cook onion, bell pepper and garlic in chicken broth over medium heat until onion is tender. Stir in tomato, beans, vinegar, cumin, red pepper and salt. Lower heat and cook uncovered until liquid is reduced, 20 minutes. Add chicken and heat to serving temperature, about 10 minutes. Serve with rice.

¼ cup diced onion
¼ cup diced red bell pepper
1 clove garlic, minced
1 cup chicken broth
1 tomato, peeled and diced
1 can (15 ounces) black beans, rinsed and drained
1 tablespoon vinegar
1 teaspoon ground cumin
½ teaspoon crushed red pepper
Salt, to taste
2 chicken breast halves, baked
Rice

SERVINGS
4

# CHICKEN PICATTA

Mix flour, salt, pepper, nutmeg and marjoram in a shallow dish. Whisk egg with water in a shallow dish. Combine bread crumbs and cheese in a third dish. Coat chicken lightly with flour mixture, then egg, then crumb mixture. Brown chicken in butter and oil over medium heat, 4 to 5 minutes per side, turning once. Remove from skillet and keep warm. Pour wine into skillet and deglaze pan, stirring to make a thin sauce. Add capers to sauce and pour over chicken. Garnish with lemon wedges.

⅓ cup all-purpose flour
½ teaspoon salt
⅛ teaspoon white pepper
⅛ teaspoon ground nutmeg
⅛ teaspoon dried marjoram
1 egg
1 tablespoon water
½ cup dry bread crumbs
⅓ cup freshly grated Parmesan cheese
4 chicken breast halves, skinned, boned and pounded thin
¼ cup butter
2 tablespoons olive oil
¾ cup dry white wine
2 tablespoons capers (optional)
Lemon wedges for garnish

SERVINGS 4

# Chic Chicken

- ¼ pound fresh mushrooms, cut into halves
- 2 tablespoons olive oil, divided
- 4 large chicken breast halves, skinned and boned
- 1 tablespoon Italian seasoning
- ½ teaspoon salt
- 1 teaspoon chicken bouillon granules
- 1 teaspoon cornstarch
- ¾ cup water
- 1 can (14 ounces) artichoke hearts, drained and cut into quarters
- Freshly grated Parmesan cheese

Sauté mushrooms in 1 tablespoon olive oil until mushrooms are tender, 5 to 8 minutes. Remove to small bowl and set aside. Sprinkle chicken breasts with Italian seasoning and salt. In same skillet, heat 1 tablespoon olive oil and cook chicken breasts until juices run clear when chicken is pierced with a fork, 8 to 10 minutes. Remove chicken to individual plates or a shallow serving dish and keep warm.

Stir together bouillon, cornstarch and water until smooth. Pour into skillet and cook over high heat, stirring constantly until sauce thickens. Add artichoke hearts and mushrooms. Stir until thoroughly heated. Spoon mixture over chicken and sprinkle with cheese.

SERVINGS 8

# Another Chicken

- 2 chicken breast halves, skinned and boned
- 3 tablespoons cornstarch, divided
- ¼ cup soy sauce, divided
- 1 teaspoon granulated sugar
- 1 clove garlic, minced
- ⅔ cup water
- ¼ cup vegetable oil
- 1 large carrot, julienned
- 20 fresh snow peas
- 1 red bell pepper, julienned
- ¼ pound fresh mushrooms, sliced
- 1 bunch green onions, thinly sliced
- Brown rice

Cut chicken into small pieces. Whisk 2 tablespoons cornstarch, 2 tablespoons soy sauce, sugar and garlic until smooth. Combine with chicken and let stand for 30 minutes. Whisk remaining cornstarch, soy sauce and water until smooth. Set aside. Heat 2 tablespoons oil in wok until hot. Add chicken and stir-fry for 4 minutes. Remove and set aside. Heat remaining oil, add vegetables and stir-fry for 1 minute. Return chicken to wok, add soy sauce mixture and cook until sauce thickens. Serve over rice.

SERVINGS
8

# Chicken Cacciatore

Brown chicken in oil until golden on all sides, 8 to 10 minutes. Combine remaining ingredients in a Dutch oven. Add chicken and simmer uncovered for 1½ to 2 hours. Remove bay leaves. Serve sauce over pasta.

- 5 to 6 pounds chicken pieces
- 6 tablespoons olive oil
- 1 can (16 ounces) tomato sauce
- 2 cans (14½ ounces each) tomatoes, or 3 cups fresh diced tomatoes
- 1 cup diced onion
- ¾ cup diced green bell pepper
- 2 cloves garlic, minced
- ½ cup Chianti or hearty red wine
- 1 tablespoon salt
- ½ teaspoon black pepper
- ½ teaspoon dried thyme
- ½ teaspoon ground allspice
- Pinch of ground red pepper
- 2 bay leaves
- 16 ounces fettuccine, cooked al dente and drained

Good friends, good food, good wine and good weather- doth a good picnic make.

*Anonymous*

Anonymous was a woman.

*Virginia Woolf*

SERVINGS 10

# Artichoke Chicken Casserole

Preheat oven to 350 degrees. Cut chicken into large pieces. Place pasta in bottom of 13 x 9-inch casserole dish. Arrange chicken, carrots and artichokes over top of pasta. Season with salt and pepper. Melt butter in saucepan. Blend in flour and cook for 2 minutes, stirring constantly. Gradually add chicken broth and stir until thickened. Remove pan from heat. Add wine, cheddar cheese, Swiss cheese, onions and ¼ cup Parmesan cheese. Pour over chicken and pasta. Combine bread crumbs, thyme and 2 tablespoons Parmesan cheese. Sprinkle over top of casserole and bake uncovered for 20 to 25 minutes. Remove from oven and sprinkle with parsley.

8 chicken breast halves, cooked, skinned and boned
6 ounces fettuccine, broken, cooked al dente and drained
4 carrots, sliced and steamed
2 cans (14 ounces each) artichokes, drained and cut into quarters
Salt and freshly ground pepper, to taste
⅓ cup butter
¼ cup all-purpose flour
2½ cups chicken broth
⅓ cup dry white wine
2 cups (8 ounces) grated cheddar cheese
2 cups (8 ounces) grated Swiss cheese
6 green onions, thinly sliced
¼ cup freshly grated Parmesan cheese
½ cup dry bread crumbs
1 tablespoon dried thyme
2 tablespoon freshly grated Parmesan cheese
2 tablespoons minced fresh parsley

SERVINGS
16-20

# CHICKEN TETRAZZINI

2 chickens
1 onion, cut into quarters
1 bay leaf
1 cup butter
1 pound fresh mushrooms, thinly sliced
1 bunch green onions, thinly sliced
4 cups half-and-half
3 tablespoons dry sherry
¼ cup white wine
2 tablespoons dried parsley
2 jars (2 ounces each) chopped pimiento
2 teaspoons salt
½ teaspoon black pepper
¼ cup butter, melted
¼ cup all-purpose flour
2 cans (4 ounces each) sliced water chestnuts
1 package (15 ounces) linguine
1 package (16 ounces) frozen peas
1 cup freshly grated Parmesan cheese

Place chicken, onion and bay leaf in a large stock pot and cover with salted water. Simmer until tender, about 45 minutes. Remove chicken and allow to cool. Discard bay leaf and reserve chicken broth. Skin and bone chicken and cut into small pieces. Set aside.

In a 5-quart Dutch oven melt 1 cup butter and sauté mushrooms for 3 to 5 minutes. Add green onions, half-and-half, sherry, wine, parsley, pimiento, salt and pepper. Heat, but do not boil. Blend ¼ cup butter and flour to make a smooth paste. Stir into mixture, add chicken and water chestnuts. Continue to stir until smooth and thickened.

Preheat oven to 375 degrees. Bring reserved chicken broth to a boil, add pasta and cook until tender. (If necessary, add water to make enough cooking liquid.) Drain and combine with chicken mixture. Stir in frozen peas. Divide mixture into two 13 x 9-inch casserole dishes and top with cheese. Bake for 20 minutes or until thoroughly heated.

SERVINGS 8-10

# ENCHILADAS CON POLLO

Preheat oven to 425 degrees. Grease a 13x9-inch casserole dish. Melt butter, add flour, stir until smooth and cook for 1 minute. Gradually whisk in chicken broth and water. Cook over medium heat, stirring until thickened. Stir in sour cream, green chilies, salt and pepper. Pour half the sauce in bottom of prepared pan. Soften tortillas in microwave for 10 seconds. Combine chicken, 2 cups cheese and ½ cup onions. Place ½ cup of chicken mixture on each tortilla. Roll up and place in baking dish seam side down. Pour remaining sauce over top. Bake uncovered for 20 minutes. Sprinkle with remaining cheese and onions. Bake for 5 minutes.

**¼ cup butter**
**¼ cup all-purpose flour**
**1 can (14½ ounces) chicken broth**
**¾ cup water**
**1 cup sour cream**
**1 can (4½ ounces) chopped green chilies**
**Salt and freshly ground pepper, to taste**
**12 flour tortillas (8-inch)**
**4 cups cooked, diced chicken breast**
**4 cups (16 ounces) grated Monterey Jack cheese, divided**
**1 bunch green onions, thinly sliced**

SERVINGS 4

# HERB CHICKEN GRILL

Mash shallot, garlic and herbs until well blended. Place in a large bowl and combine with salt, lemon, wine and olive oil. Add chicken, cover and chill for 8 to 24 hours. Remove chicken from marinade. Grill chicken over medium coals until done, 10 minutes per side.

**1 shallot, minced**
**3 cloves garlic, minced**
**1 tablespoon minced fresh rosemary**
**1 tablespoon minced fresh thyme**
**1 tablespoon minced fresh oregano**
**1 tablespoon minced fresh basil**
**1 teaspoon salt**
**1 lemon, thinly sliced**
**1 cup dry white wine**
**½ cup olive oil**
**2 to 3 pounds assorted chicken pieces**

SERVINGS
4

# Grilled Chicken with Tomato Pepper Salsa

Whisk vinegar, lime juice and oil until well blended. Add rosemary, basil, tomato, salt and pepper and stir until blended. Pour marinade over chicken, cover and chill for 1 hour. Remove chicken from marinade and grill over medium coals until done, 2 to 3 minutes per side. Spoon salsa over warm chicken and serve immediately.

Tomato Pepper Salsa: Sauté onion in oil until tender, about 5 minutes. Add bell peppers, jalapeño peppers, salt and pepper and sauté for 2 to 4 minutes, stirring occasionally. Add lime juice, rosemary, basil and tomatoes and sauté until thoroughly heated, 2 to 3 minutes.

1/3 cup rice wine vinegar
1/4 cup lime juice
1/4 cup olive oil
2 tablespoons minced fresh rosemary
4 fresh basil leaves, minced
1 tomato, diced
Salt and freshly ground pepper, to taste
4 chicken breast halves, skinned, boned and pounded thin

TOMATO PEPPER SALSA:
1/2 small onion, sliced
1/4 cup olive oil
1 yellow bell pepper, sliced
1/2 red bell pepper, sliced
2 jalapeño peppers, seeded and diced
1/4 teaspoon salt
1/8 teaspoon black pepper
2 tablespoons fresh lime juice
1 tablespoon minced fresh rosemary
2 fresh basil leaves, minced
3 tomatoes, diced

**Only the mediocre are always at their best.**

*Jean Giraudoux*

SERVINGS
2

# PHEASANT MARSALA

Remove breast and thigh meat from bone then cut into small pieces. Cover with buttermilk and chill for at least 2 hours. Bring water and ½ teaspoon salt to a boil. Add wings and drumsticks, cover and simmer for 2 hours. Discard wings and drumsticks. Boil stock until reduced to 1 cup. Set aside. Combine flour, remaining salt and pepper. Coat pheasant pieces with flour mixture. Melt 2 tablespoons butter in a Dutch oven and brown pheasant until golden. Remove and set aside. Heat remaining butter in same pan and sauté mushrooms and shallot. Add stock and wine and deglaze pan. Return pheasant to pan and simmer covered for 1 hour. Serve over rice or wild rice.

**1 pheasant**
**1 cup buttermilk**
**2 cups water**
**1 teaspoon salt, divided**
**½ cup all-purpose flour**
**¼ teaspoon black pepper**
**¼ cup butter, divided**
**¼ pound fresh mushrooms, sliced**
**1 shallot, minced**
**1 cup Marsala wine**
**Rice or wild rice**

SERVINGS
2

# Grilled Turkey with Fresh Peach Salsa

Whisk vinegar, lime juice, oil, honey and jalapeño pepper until well blended. Marinate turkey in zippered plastic bag and chill for at least 2 hours, turning several times. Grill tenderloin over medium coals until done, 15 to 20 minutes. Slice tenderloin and serve with salsa.

Fresh Peach Salsa: Whisk lime juice, oil and salt until well blended. Stir in remaining ingredients. Cover and chill for 2 hours.

**1/3 cup red wine vinegar**
**Juice of 1 lime**
**1/4 cup vegetable oil**
**2 tablespoons honey**
**1 jalapeño pepper, seeded and minced**
**1 turkey breast tenderloin (about 8 ounces)**

**FRESH PEACH SALSA:**
**Juice of 1 lime**
**1/4 cup vegetable oil**
**1/2 teaspoon salt**
**1 large ripe peach, peeled and diced**
**1 tomatillo, husked and diced**
**1/3 cup diced red bell pepper**
**1 tablespoon diced red onion**
**1 jalapeño pepper, seeded and minced**
**2 tablespoons minced fresh cilantro**

**The cardiologist's diet: If it tastes good, spit it out.**

*Paulina Borsook*

SERVINGS
4-6

# SPRING PAELLA

Sauté onion and garlic in oil in a 5-quart Dutch oven over medium heat until tender. Stir in rice, chicken broth, carrots, tomato, thyme, saffron, salt and red pepper. Bring to a boil, reduce heat, cover and simmer for 15 minutes. Layer chicken and shrimp over rice mixture. Cover and cook until chicken is no longer pink, 10 to 15 minutes. Cook asparagus and zucchini in a medium saucepan until crisp tender, about 5 minutes. Drain and layer vegetables over chicken and shrimp. Cover and remove from heat. Let stand for 10 minutes then gently stir. Serve on a large, warmed platter.

**1 large onion, diced**
**1 or 2 cloves garlic, minced**
**2 teaspoons olive oil**
**1 cup long-grain white rice**
**1 can (14 ounces) chicken broth**
**2 carrots, cut diagonally**
**1 large tomato, diced**
**1 teaspoon dried thyme**
**½ teaspoon saffron**
**½ teaspoon salt**
**Pinch of ground red pepper**
**2 chicken breast halves, skinned, boned and cut into 1½-inch pieces**
**½ pound large shrimp, shelled and deveined**
**½ pound fresh asparagus spears, cut into 1-inch pieces**
**1 medium zucchini, sliced**

SERVINGS
6-8

# Turkey Tenderloins with Raspberry Glaze

Stir jam, vinegar, mustard, orange zest and thyme together. Bring to a boil and cook, stirring until liquid is reduced by one-fourth, 2 to 3 minutes. Reserve ½ cup glaze. Brush turkey with remaining glaze and place on rack in broiler pan. Broil about 4 inches from heat, turning and basting once with glaze. Cook until meat is no longer pink in center, 8 to 10 minutes. Slice and serve with reserved glaze.

**½ cup seedless raspberry jam**
**6 tablespoons raspberry vinegar**
**¼ cup Dijon mustard**
**1 teaspoon grated orange zest**
**½ teaspoon dried thyme**
**4 turkey tenderloins, 8 ounces each**

I have always thought that
there is no more fruitful
source of family discontent
than badly cooked
dinners and untidy ways.

*Mrs. Isabella Beeton*

SERVINGS
6

# Poached Salmon with Two Sauces

Bring fish stock to a boil and add lemon juice, pickling spice, salt, celery and parsley. Add fillets and reduce heat until stock is simmering. Cover surface with parchment paper and simmer until fish is opaque and firm, for 6 to 8 minutes. Remove fillets from liquid and carefully remove skin. Serve with desired sauce.

Raspberry Sauce: Heat fruit spread until melted. Add raspberries. Serve sauce warm.

Beurre Blanc: In a large saucepan boil shallots and wine over medium heat until ¼ cup liquid remains. Add 1 cup cream and boil, whisking constantly, until reduced by half. Add remaining cream and boil until mixture becomes thick. About 1½ cups liquid should remain. Remove pan from heat and whisk in butter a little at a time. Sauce should have a smooth consistency. It may be necessary to warm pan slightly to melt butter, but do not let sauce boil. Season with salt and pepper. To keep sauce warm until serving, place over a pan of hot water.

*Fish stock is available in cube form at specialty stores.*

3 cups fish stock or white wine
2 teaspoons lemon juice
2 teaspoons mixed pickling spice
1 teaspoon salt
1 stalk celery with leaves, cut in pieces
1 sprig parsley
6 salmon fillets, 6 ounces each

RASPBERRY SAUCE:
1 jar (10 ounces) seedless raspberry fruit spread
1½ pints fresh raspberries

BEURRE BLANC:
3 large shallots, minced
1½ cups dry white wine
2 cups heavy cream
1 cup unsalted butter, cut in ½-inch cubes, softened
Salt and freshly ground white pepper, to taste

SERVINGS
6

# Spinach Stuffed Salmon

Heat butter in a saucepan over medium heat. Whisk in flour and cook for 3 minutes. Add warm milk and stir until smooth and thick. Stir in herbs, salt and pepper. Remove from heat, add cheese and sherry and stir until smooth. Microwave spinach until wilted, 3 minutes. Cool and squeeze dry. Melt butter and sauté mushrooms and shallots for 10 minutes over medium heat. Add spinach and cook until warm. Stir in cheese sauce. Cover and chill until filling has cooled completely, about 1 hour. With kitchen tweezers, remove all bones from salmon. Carefully cut a slit lengthwise in side of salmon to form a pocket. Place in a 13x9-inch baking dish and fill pocket with stuffing. (Salmon may be prepared and chilled up to 4 hours before cooking.)

Preheat oven to 425 degrees. Pour wine around salmon, squeeze lemon over top and sprinkle with bread crumbs. Bake until center of salmon is opaque and flakes easily, 20 to 30 minutes.

1 tablespoon butter
1 tablespoon all-purpose flour
6 tablespoons warm milk
½ teaspoon dried basil
¼ teaspoon dried oregano
⅛ teaspoon dried thyme
¼ teaspoon salt
Pinch of white pepper
¼ cup freshly grated Parmesan cheese
1 tablespoon dry sherry
½ pound fresh spinach, stems removed
¼ cup butter
¼ pound fresh mushrooms, diced
3 ounces shallots, minced
2½ to 3 pound salmon fillet, center cut
1 cup white wine
1 lemon
½ cup buttered bread crumbs

**Some wines improve with age. But only if the grapes were good in the first place.**

*Abigail Van Buren*

SERVINGS 6

# Grilled Salmon with Cucumber Dill Sauce

Brush salmon lightly with oil and grill over medium coals until fish is opaque and flakes easily, 4 minutes per side. Serve with sauce.

Cucumber Dill Sauce: Mix sour cream, cucumber, onion, dill, vinegar, salt and red pepper together. Cover and chill.

6 salmon steaks
Vegetable oil
CUCUMBER DILL SAUCE:
2 cups sour cream
1 cucumber, peeled, seeded and diced
1 tablespoon grated onion
1 tablespoon snipped fresh dill
1 tablespoon white wine vinegar
1 teaspoon salt
Pinch of ground red pepper

SERVINGS 4

# Baked Roughy with Artichoke Hearts

Preheat oven to 350 degrees. Cut fillets into serving size pieces and place in a baking dish. Sauté onion, celery, tomatoes and artichoke hearts in butter. Add wine and bay leaf and cook for 3 minutes. Pour sauce over fish. Cover and bake for 15 minutes. Uncover and bake for 5 minutes. Discard bay leaf and sprinkle with cheese.

2 pounds orange roughy fillets
½ medium onion, diced
2 stalks celery, diced
½ cup diced tomatoes
1 can (14 ounces) artichoke hearts, drained and cut into quarters
1 tablespoon butter
½ cup white wine or juice of ½ lemon
Bay leaf
¼ cup freshly grated Parmesan cheese

SERVINGS 6

# Snapper Martinique

Sauté onion and garlic in butter. Add tomatoes, sugar, oregano and basil and simmer for 10 minutes. Season to taste and set aside.

Slice bananas in half lengthwise then halve each piece. Sauté in 2 tablespoons butter over medium heat until lightly browned, 2 minutes per side. Transfer to a platter and place in a warm oven. In a small bowl combine Worcestershire sauce, 2 tablespoons lemon juice, salt and pepper. In a separate bowl whisk together eggs and milk. Rub fish with Worcestershire mixture then coat with flour. Dip fillets in egg mixture and pan fry in ½ cup oil over medium heat for about 4 minutes per side. Arrange fish on top of warm bananas and cover with sauce. Drain oil from skillet and melt remaining butter. Add parsley and 2 tablespoons lemon juice. Drizzle over fish and serve immediately.

**⅓ cup diced onion**
**1 clove garlic, minced**
**2 tablespoons butter**
**2 cups tomatoes, peeled, seeded and diced**
**¼ teaspoon granulated sugar**
**¼ teaspoon dried oregano**
**¼ teaspoon dried basil**
**Salt and freshly ground pepper, to taste**
**4 small bananas**
**½ cup butter, divided**
**1 teaspoon Worcestershire sauce**
**¼ cup fresh lemon juice, divided**
**1 teaspoon salt**
**¼ teaspoon white pepper**
**2 large eggs**
**2 tablespoons milk**
**2 pounds red snapper or other firm white fish, cut into serving size pieces**
**¾ cup all-purpose flour**
**½ cup vegetable oil**
**1 tablespoon minced fresh parsley**

**I'm fond of anything that comes out of the sea, and that includes sailors.**

*Janet Flanner*

SERVINGS 4

# ZESTY GRILLED SWORDFISH

Whisk soy sauce, orange juice, oil, ketchup, garlic, parsley, lemon juice, oregano and pepper until well blended. Brush marinade over fish steaks, cover and chill for up to 4 hours. Grill or broil for 4 to 5 minutes per side, turning once.

- 2 tablespoons soy sauce
- 2 tablespoons orange juice
- 1 tablespoon vegetable oil
- 1 tablespoon ketchup
- 3 cloves garlic, minced
- 2 tablespoons minced fresh parsley
- ½ teaspoon lemon juice
- ¼ teaspoon dried oregano
- ¼ teaspoon freshly ground black pepper
- 2 pounds swordfish steaks, sliced 1 inch thick

SERVINGS 8

# LEMON SOY TUNA STEAKS

Whisk together onion, soy sauce, lemon zest, lemon juice, garlic, mustard and oil. Pour over fish and pierce each steak several times with a fork. Turn fish and pierce again. Cover and chill for 1 to 6 hours. Grill or broil fish for 5 to 6 minutes per side, basting often with remaining marinade. (Allow 10 minutes total cooking time for each inch thickness of steaks.) Garnish with lemon or lime wedges and parsley.

*Halibut steaks or swordfish steaks may be substituted for tuna steaks.*

- ¼ cup diced onion
- ⅓ cup soy sauce
- 1 teaspoon grated lemon zest
- ¼ cup fresh lemon juice
- 1 clove garlic, minced
- 2 teaspoons Dijon mustard
- ½ cup vegetable oil
- 8 tuna steaks, 6 ounces each
- Lemon or lime wedges for garnish
- ¼ cup minced fresh parsley

SERVINGS 4

# SEAFOOD KABOBS

Whisk lime juice, olive oil, garlic, dill, salt and pepper until well blended. Marinate fish, shrimp, scallops and bell peppers for 20 to 30 minutes, turning several times. Skewer fish and vegetables and grill over medium coals for 2½ minutes per side. Serve over rice.

3 tablespoons fresh lime juice
6 tablespoons olive oil
1 clove garlic, minced
1 tablespoon snipped fresh dill
½ teaspoon salt
1 teaspoon black pepper
¾ pound swordfish or tuna steaks, cut into 1½-inch pieces
4 jumbo shrimp
4 large scallops
1 red bell pepper, cut into eighths
1 green bell pepper, cut into eighths
Rice

SERVINGS 4

# SHRIMP PIZAZZI

Sauté zucchini and bell pepper in olive oil until lightly browned. Add shrimp, garlic and seasonings and cook until shrimp are opaque. Stir in tomatoes and lemon juice. Cook until mixture is thoroughly heated, 2 minutes. Season to taste and serve over rice.

1 medium zucchini, julienned
1 medium red bell pepper, julienned
3 tablespoons olive oil
1 pound shrimp, shelled and deveined
3 cloves garlic, minced
½ to 1 teaspoon crushed red pepper
1½ teaspoons dried thyme
1 cup plum tomatoes, drained and diced
Juice of ½ lemon
Salt and freshly ground pepper, to taste
Rice

SERVINGS

4-6

# SHRIMP ÉTOUFFÉE

Combine salt, red pepper (less for the fainthearted!), white pepper, black pepper, basil and thyme in a small bowl and set aside. Combine onion, celery and bell pepper and set aside. In a large heavy skillet heat oil over high heat until almost smoking, about 4 minutes. Using a metal whisk, slowly stir in flour until smooth. Cook, stirring constantly, until flour (roux) is dark reddish brown, about 5 minutes. Be very careful not to scorch roux. Remove skillet from heat, add vegetables and 1 tablespoon of dry seasoning mixture. Continue to stir until cool, about 5 minutes.

Bring 2 cups of fish stock to a boil. Gradually add vegetable mixture and whisk until dissolved. Reduce heat and simmer, stirring constantly until mixture thickens. Remove from heat and set aside. In a large saucepan melt half the butter and sauté shrimp and 1 cup green onions for 1 minute. Add remaining butter and fish stock. Do not stir mixture but shake back and forth constantly. Cook until butter melts and combines with shrimp, 4 to 6 minutes. Stir in vegetable mixture and remaining dry seasonings. Remove from heat. (If étouffée begins to separate add 1 tablespoon of fish stock or water and shake pan until mixture combines.) Serve in warm shallow bowls over rice and garnish with remaining green onions.

**2 teaspoons salt**
**2 teaspoons ground red pepper**
**1 teaspoon white pepper**
**1 teaspoon black pepper**
**1 teaspoon dried basil**
**½ teaspoon dried thyme**
**¼ cup diced white onion**
**¼ cup diced celery**
**¼ cup diced green bell pepper**
**7 tablespoons vegetable oil**
**¾ cup all-purpose flour**
**3 cups fish stock, divided**
**1 cup unsalted butter, divided**
**2 pounds medium shrimp, peeled and deveined**
**1¼ cups thinly sliced green onions, divided**
**Rice**

SERVINGS
4

# FETTUCCINE WITH CLAM SAUCE

Sauté garlic in oil, mashing to extract flavor. Add liquid from clams, parsley, chives, oregano and pepper. Simmer for 5 minutes, stir in clams and cook for 8 to 10 minutes to reduce liquid. To serve, spoon over fettuccine and sprinkle with cheese.

2 cloves garlic, sliced
2 tablespoons olive oil
2 cans ($7\frac{1}{2}$ ounces each) minced clams, reserve liquid
½ cup minced fresh parsley
½ cup snipped fresh chives
½ teaspoon dried oregano
Coarsely ground black pepper, to taste
8 ounces fettuccine, cooked al dente and drained
Freshly grated Parmesan cheese

I feel a recipe is only a theme, which an intelligent cook can play each time with a variation

 *Jehane Benoît*

SERVINGS 4

# SZECHUAN SHRIMP

Combine ketchup, sherry, sugar, soy sauce and 1½ tablespoons oil. Set aside. Whisk water and cornstarch until smooth. Heat 2 tablespoons oil in a wok or skillet until hot. Sauté snow peas, onions, bamboo shoots, ginger root, garlic and hot pepper sauce for 1 to 2 minutes. Add shrimp and sauté for 1 minute. Stir in ketchup mixture and simmer until shrimp is no longer pink. Add cornstarch mixture and stir until thickened. Serve over rice.

- ⅓ cup ketchup
- 3 tablespoons dry sherry
- 2 tablespoons granulated sugar
- 1 tablespoon soy sauce
- 3½ tablespoons sesame oil, divided
- 3 tablespoons water
- 1 tablespoon cornstarch
- 1 cup fresh snow peas, strings removed
- ½ cup thinly sliced green onions
- ½ cup bamboo shoots
- 1 tablespoon minced fresh ginger root
- 3 large cloves garlic, minced
- ½ teaspoon hot pepper sauce
- 1 pound medium shrimp, peeled and deveined
- Rice

**Flops are a part of life's menu and I'm not one to miss out on any of the courses.**

*Rosalind Russell*

SERVINGS 6

# Salmon Primavera

1 cup fish stock or chicken broth
½ cup dry white wine
½ onion, cut into quarters
2 stalks celery, cut into halves
1 teaspoon salt
¼ teaspoon black pepper
1 pound salmon fillets
1 pound fresh asparagus spears, cut diagonally into 1-inch pieces
1 small zucchini, julienned
½ pound fresh mushrooms, sliced
2 cloves garlic, minced
1 bunch green onions, thinly sliced
2 tablespoons butter
3 tablespoons all-purpose flour
1 cup warm milk
½ teaspoon dried basil
¼ teaspoon dried oregano
Pinch of white pepper
¼ cup freshly grated Parmesan cheese
Juice and zest of 1 lemon
1 cup frozen green peas, thawed
1 tomato, peeled, seeded and diced
12 ounces penne pasta, cooked al dente and drained

Bring fish stock, wine, onion, celery, salt and pepper to a boil in a large saucepan. Add salmon, cover surface with parchment paper and reduce heat. Cook until salmon is opaque and flakes easily with a fork, 5 to 10 minutes. Remove salmon to a plate. Reserve cooking liquid and discard vegetables. Cool salmon slightly, remove skin and cut into bite size pieces.

Cook asparagus and zucchini until crisp tender. Immediately rinse in cold water. Set aside. Sauté mushrooms, garlic and green onions in butter until liquid is reduced. Sprinkle with flour and cook for 2 minutes. Add milk and reserved poaching liquid. Stir until mixture thickens. Add remaining seasonings, cheese, lemon juice and zest. Stir in peas, tomato, salmon, asparagus and zucchini. Heat thoroughly, pour over cooked pasta and toss gently.

SERVINGS 4-6

# ORECCHIETTE DEL MAR

Sauté shrimp in oil for 1 minute in a large skillet over medium heat. Add scallops, garlic and onions and sauté for 2 minutes. Add remaining ingredients except cheese and heat for 3 to 5 minutes, stirring gently. Pour sauce over pasta and toss. Sprinkle with grated cheese and serve immediately.

- ½ pound shrimp, shelled and deveined
- 1 tablespoon olive oil
- ½ pound sea scallops, sliced into ¼-inch rounds
- 3 cloves garlic, minced
- ½ cup sliced green onions
- 2 cups frozen peas, thawed
- 2 cups fresh tomatoes, peeled and diced
- ½ cup white wine
- 1 tablespoon minced fresh basil or 1 teaspoon dried basil
- ½ teaspoon dried oregano
- Salt and freshly ground pepper, to taste
- ¼ cup minced fresh parsley
- 8 ounces orecchiette or small shell pasta, cooked al dente and drained
- Freshly grated Parmesan or Romano cheese

SERVINGS 4

# PASTA WITH PROSCIUTTO

Cook asparagus until crisp tender, immediately rinse in cold water and set aside. Melt 6 tablespoons butter in a large pan, add prosciutto and tomatoes with liquid and cook until slightly thickened, 2 to 3 minutes. Reduce heat to low and add pasta, 2 tablespoons butter, cheese and asparagus. Stir until butter and cheese are melted.

- 1 pound fresh asparagus spears, cut into 1-inch pieces
- ½ cup unsalted butter, divided
- ¼ pound prosciutto ham, thinly sliced and cut into strips
- 1 can (14½ ounces) plum tomatoes with liquid, diced
- 8 ounces fresh angel hair pasta, cooked al dente and drained
- ½ cup freshly grated Parmesan cheese

SERVINGS
6

# CHICKEN AGAIN!

Preheat oven to 375 degrees. Grease a 2-quart casserole dish. Sauté mushrooms in butter. Combine soup, half-and-half and wine in a large bowl until well blended. Add linguine, mushrooms and chicken and mix gently. Spread mixture in prepared dish. Top with cheese and bake until bubbly, 25 minutes.

- ¼ pound fresh mushrooms, sliced
- 2 tablespoons butter
- 1 can (10 ¾ ounces) cream of mushroom soup
- ½ cup half-and-half
- 2 tablespoons white wine or dry sherry
- 2 cups cooked, diced chicken or turkey
- 8 ounces linguine, cooked al dente and drained
- ⅓ cup freshly grated Parmesan cheese

I was always eager
to salt a good stew.
The trouble was that
I was expected to supply
the meat and potatoes as well.

*Bette Davis*

SERVINGS
10-12

# Pastitsio

Meat Sauce: Cook onion, garlic, bay leaf and oregano in oil until onion is tender, 5 to 8 minutes. Add lamb and cook over moderate heat until lamb is no longer pink, stirring to break up lumps. Stir in wine, tomato paste, tomatoes with liquid and salt. Bring mixture to a boil and simmer covered for 20 to 25 minutes, stirring occasionally. Remove from heat and discard bay leaf. Stir in parsley and allow to cool while making white sauce.

White sauce: Melt butter in a saucepan over medium heat. Whisk in flour until smooth. Slowly add milk, stirring until mixture reaches a boil. Reduce heat and simmer, stirring for 2 minutes. Add nutmeg, cinnamon, salt and pepper.

Preheat oven to 350 degrees. Grease a 13 x 9-inch casserole dish. Combine pasta, ⅔ cup Parmesan cheese, butter, feta cheese and 2 lightly beaten eggs. Spread half of the pasta mixture in prepared dish. Stir 2 lightly beaten eggs into meat sauce and spread over pasta. Layer remaining pasta over meat sauce. Whisk 1 egg into white sauce, pour over pasta and smooth with back of spoon to cover completely. Sprinkle with remaining Parmesan cheese and bread crumbs. Bake on center rack until golden, 40 to 45 minutes. Allow casserole to stand for 15 minutes. Cut into squares and serve.

**MEAT SAUCE:**
**1 cup finely diced onion**
**1 clove garlic, minced**
**1 bay leaf**
**½ teaspoon dried oregano**
**2 tablespoons olive oil**
**1 pound ground lamb**
**½ cup dry red wine**
**2 tablespoons tomato paste**
**1 can (28 ounces) plum tomatoes with liquid, diced**
**1 teaspoon salt**
**⅓ cup minced fresh parsley leaves**
**WHITE SAUCE:**
**¼ cup unsalted butter**
**¼ cup all-purpose flour**
**3 cups milk**
**¼ teaspoon ground nutmeg**
**¼ teaspoon ground cinnamon**
**Salt and freshly ground pepper, to taste**
**16 ounces ziti or penne pasta, cooked al dente and drained**
**1 cup freshly grated Parmesan cheese, divided**
**½ cup butter, softened**
**4 ounces feta cheese, crumbled**
**5 large eggs, divided**
**⅓ cup dry bread crumbs**

SERVINGS
6-8

# Cannelloni with Balsamella Sauce

Sauté onion and garlic in oil until tender, 5 to 8 minutes. Add spinach and cook until moisture evaporates. Place in a large mixing bowl and set aside. In same skillet crumble and brown meat in 1 tablespoon butter. Drain and add to spinach mixture. Heat remaining butter and sauté chicken livers about 5 minutes. Chop livers and add to spinach mixture. Cool slightly and add cheese, eggs, cream, oregano, salt and pepper and mix well.

Preheat oven to 375 degrees. Pour tomato sauce into a 13 x 9-inch casserole dish. Stuff manicotti sleeves with filling and arrange in dish. Pour Balsamella Sauce over manicotti sleeves and top with cheese. Bake for 20 minutes or until sauce bubbles.

Balsamella Sauce: Melt butter in saucepan, whisk in flour and cook for 2 minutes. Remove from heat and add milk, cream, salt and white pepper. Return to heat and whisk until sauce thickens.

**FILLING:**
- 1/4 cup diced onion
- 1 teaspoon minced garlic
- 2 tablespoons olive oil
- 1 package (10 ounces) frozen chopped spinach, thawed and squeezed dry
- 1 pound ground round
- 2 tablespoons butter, divided
- 2 chicken livers (optional)
- 1/4 cup freshly grated Parmesan cheese
- 2 eggs, lightly beaten
- 2 tablespoons heavy cream
- 1/2 teaspoon dried oregano
- 1 teaspoon salt
- 1/4 teaspoon black pepper
- 1 can (15 ounces) tomato sauce
- 1 package (8 ounces) manicotti sleeves, cooked al dente and drained
- 1/4 cup freshly grated parmesan cheese

**BALSAMELLA SAUCE:**
- 3 tablespoons butter
- 3 tablespoons all-purpose flour
- 3/4 cup milk
- 3/4 cup heavy cream
- 1/2 teaspoon salt
- 1/4 teaspoon white pepper

SERVINGS
6

# Asparagus Mushroom Pasta

Cook asparagus until crisp tender, immediately rinse in cold water and set aside. In a large saucepan sauté mushrooms and garlic in butter until tender, about 5 minutes. Remove from pan with slotted spoon and set aside. Add flour to liquid in pan and cook until thickened, about 4 minutes. Whisk in wine. Stir in half-and-half, salt and pepper. Heat thoroughly but do not boil. Stir in asparagus, mushrooms and cheese. Gently toss with linguine and serve immediately.

1 pound fresh asparagus spears, cut into 1-inch pieces
1 pound fresh mushrooms, sliced
2 cloves garlic, minced
½ cup butter
2 tablespoons all-purpose flour
⅓ cup dry white wine
2 cups half-and-half
½ teaspoon salt
½ teaspoon black pepper
½ cup freshly grated Parmesan cheese
12 ounces linguine, cooked al dente and drained

SERVINGS
4-6

# Zucchini Ziti

Sauté onion, garlic and zucchini in oil for 3 to 5 minutes. Drain tomatoes, reserving liquid. Add enough water to tomato juice to make 1½ cups. Moisten flour with 3 tablespoons tomato liquid to make a paste. Stir paste into liquid and then stir into zucchini. Cut tomatoes in quarters and add to skillet along with oregano, basil and salt. Cover and simmer for 15 to 20 minutes, stirring occasionally. Toss pasta with sauce and sprinkle with cheese.

½ medium onion, diced
2 cloves garlic, minced
1 medium zucchini, thinly sliced
2 tablespoons olive oil
1 can (14½ ounces) whole tomatoes, reserve liquid
2 tablespoons all-purpose flour
1 teaspoon dried oregano
1 teaspoon dried basil
½ teaspoon salt
8 ounces ziti pasta, cooked al dente and drained
¼ cup freshly grated Parmesan cheese

SERVINGS

10-12

# LASAGNA FLORENTINE

4 ounces cream cheese, softened
16 ounces ricotta cheese
¼ cup sour cream
½ teaspoon dried oregano
1 teaspoon salt
½ teaspoon black pepper
1 small onion, diced
4 cloves garlic, minced
½ cup butter
6 tablespoons all-purpose flour
3 cups hot chicken broth
12 to 15 lasagna noodles, cooked al dente and drained
2 packages (10 ounces each) frozen chopped spinach, thawed and squeezed dry
8 ounces fresh mushrooms, sliced
2 cups (8 ounces) grated mozzarella cheese
2 cups (8 ounces) grated mild cheddar cheese
½ cup freshly grated Parmesan cheese

Combine cream cheese, ricotta cheese and sour cream. Stir in oregano, salt and pepper. Set aside. Sauté onion and garlic in butter until tender, 5 to 8 minutes. Stir in flour and cook for 2 minutes. Whisk in chicken broth, blending until smooth and thickened.

Preheat oven to 325 degrees. Grease a deep 13 x 9-inch baking dish. Place one-third of the noodles in bottom of pan. Layer one-half of the cheese mixture, spinach, mushrooms, mozzarella cheese and cheddar cheese. Spoon one-third of the garlic sauce over cheese. Repeat layers. Top with remaining noodles and garlic sauce. Sprinkle with Parmesan cheese. Cover and bake for 1¼ hours. Uncover and bake for 15 minutes.

**If you accept a dinner invitation— you have a moral obligation to be amusing.**

*Wallis Simpson*

SERVINGS
4

# FARFALLE WITH WILD MUSHROOM SAUCE

Sauté mushrooms, onions and garlic in walnut oil until liquid has evaporated. Stir in wine, tarragon, salt and pepper. Remove from heat and stir in crème fraîche. Toss with pasta and top with walnuts and cheese.

- ½ pound fresh button mushrooms, sliced
- ½ pound assorted wild mushrooms, sliced (shiitake, portobello, porcini, morels)
- 1 bunch green onions, sliced
- 1 clove garlic, minced
- ¼ cup walnut oil
- ¼ cup dry white wine
- 2 teaspoons fresh tarragon
- ¼ teaspoon salt
- ⅛ teaspoon black pepper
- ½ cup crème fraîche (page 61) or sour cream
- 8 ounces farfalle pasta, cooked al dente and drained
- ¼ cup chopped walnuts, toasted
- ¼ cup freshly grated Parmesan cheese

It's always something.

*Gilda Radner*

SERVINGS
6-8

# Penne Pasta Aubergine

Sauté onion and garlic in butter and oil in a large skillet until tender. Stir in salt, bayleaf and eggplant. Cover and cook for 10 minutes, stirring occasionally. Add mushrooms, basil, bell pepper, tomatoes and tomato paste. Cover and simmer for 10 minutes. Add wine and parsley. Cover and simmer for 15 to 20 minutes. Just before serving, stir in 1 cup cheese and spoon sauce over pasta. Sprinkle with remaining cheese.

1 cup diced onion
3 cloves garlic, minced
1 tablespoon butter
1 tablespoon olive oil
1 teaspoon salt
1 bay leaf
4 cups eggplant, cubed
1 pound fresh mushrooms, diced
1 teaspoon dried basil
1 cup diced green bell pepper
2 medium tomatoes, diced
¼ cup tomato paste
1 cup Marsala wine
¼ cup minced fresh parsley
1½ cups freshly grated Parmesan cheese, divided
16 ounces penne pasta, cooked al dente and drained

SERVINGS
6-8

# Black Bean Tortilla Bake

Preheat oven to 350 degrees. Grease a 13 x 9-inch casserole dish. In a large saucepan combine onion, bell pepper, tomatoes with juice, picante sauce, garlic, cumin and hot pepper sauce. Bring to a boil, reduce heat and simmer uncovered for 10 minutes. Stir in beans. Spread a third of the mixture in prepared dish. Place 6 tortillas, overlapping as necessary, on top of beans and sprinkle with 1 cup cheese. Repeat layers and top with remaining bean mixture. Cover and bake until thoroughly heated, 30 to 35 minutes. Remove from oven, sprinkle with remaining cheese and let stand for 10 minutes. Top with tomatoes, green onions and black olives.

2 cups diced onion
1½ cups diced green bell pepper
1 can (14½ ounces) diced tomatoes, with liquid
¾ cup picante sauce
2 cloves garlic, minced
2 teaspoons ground cumin
2 cans (15 ounces each) black beans, rinsed and drained
12 corn or flour tortillas (6-inch)
3 cups (12 ounces) grated Monterey Jack cheese
2 or 3 dashes hot pepper sauce (optional)
2 tomatoes, diced
4 green onions, thinly sliced
1 can (3.8 ounces) sliced black olives, drained

# ARTISTICALLY ARRANGES ARTICHOKES

## "I think that I shall never see, an orchid lovely as a pea."

Georgia O'Keeffe may have been the ultimate sensualist. Just look at her paintings. Flowers so real your mind is filled with their fragrance. Rock formations painted as fleshy curves that seem to invite a caress. One must wonder, then, why she didn't turn her hedonistic brush to that most sensual of pleasures—food. ❖ The answer is, she did. But the consequences were so shocking that art historians still deny it. ❖ Georgia was slender beyond belief, but when she fell prey to the artistic interplay of taste and texture that makes up nature's vegetable bounty, she fell hard. Suddenly, and without explanation, landscapes, cityscapes and flowers were set aside for canvasses adorned with artichokes, asparagus and wax beans. ❖ Audiences found the paintings strangely disquieting. Storekeepers and green grocers were often overwhelmed with unmeetable demands for huge quantities of particular vegetables after an O'Keeffe showing. And the customers, they reported, "seemed possessed of a vegetable lust and would not take 'no' for an answer!" ❖ A display of several canvasses from her "Tater" Period caused such a rush on sweet potatoes that it is believed to have caused the Great Yam Famine of '29. Her single painting, "Spinach," displayed in a prominent bank lobby sent an entire town into such an embarrassing display of greens-eating abandon that, to this day, many cannot watch a Popeye cartoon. ❖ In the end, the paintings were destroyed or placed in vaults, away from innocent eyes and Ms. O'Keeffe went back to the subjects she painted so well. ❖ But we will never look at a produce section again without Georgia on our minds.

# Vegetables & Side Dishes

SERVINGS
6

# Asparagus Bundles

Preheat oven to 350 degrees. Grease a 13 x 9-inch baking dish. Cook asparagus until crisp tender, about 5 minutes. Plunge immediately into ice water to stop cooking process. Drain and pat dry. Spiral wrap each slice of prosciutto around 5 or 6 asparagus spears and place in baking dish. Sprinkle cheese across center of bundles. Season generously with pepper. Combine melted butter and garlic and drizzle over each bundle. Bake until asparagus is thoroughly heated and cheese is melted, 10 minutes.

30 to 36 fresh asparagus spears, tough ends removed
3 slices prosciutto ham, cut into halves lengthwise
¼ cup freshly grated Parmesan cheese
Freshly ground pepper, to taste
½ cup butter, melted
2 cloves garlic, minced

SERVINGS
4

# Asparagus Caesar

Preheat oven to 425 degrees. Place asparagus in shallow baking dish. Combine lemon juice and oil and drizzle over asparagus. Sprinkle with cheese and bake uncovered for 15 minutes.

1 pound fresh asparagus spears, tough ends removed
3 tablespoons fresh lemon juice
3 tablespoons olive oil
¼ cup freshly grated Parmesan cheese

SERVINGS
6

# Artful Artichokes

Remove stems, cut off top quarter of artichokes and trim leaves. Bring a large pot of water to boil and add artichokes, lemon juice and salt. Reduce heat and gently boil for 25 to 30 minutes. Drain. Remove inner leaves and fuzzy choke and pat dry. To retain shape while baking, wrap each artichoke in foil, leaving top open. Place on baking sheet.

Soufflé: Bring milk and butter to a boil. Add flour and whisk until mixture thickens. Remove from heat and whisk in egg yolks, one at a time. Add artichoke hearts, onion, cheese and seasonings. Cool to room temperature.

Preheat oven to 375 degrees. Beat egg whites until stiff. Gently fold egg whites into cooled artichoke mixture. Fill artichokes with soufflé mixture. Bake until soufflés are golden and puffed, 30 minutes. Carefully remove foil and serve immediately.

6 large artichokes
Juice of ½ lemon
1 teaspoon salt
SOUFFLÉ:
¾ cup milk
3 tablespoons butter
3 tablespoons all-purpose flour
4 eggs, separated
1 can (14 ounces) artichoke hearts, drained and chopped
1 tablespoon thinly sliced green onion
¼ cup (1 ounce) grated Gruyère cheese
Pinch of ground nutmeg
Pinch of ground red pepper
¼ teaspoon salt

Eating an artichoke is like getting to know someone really well.

*Willi Hastings*

SERVINGS
4

# Garlic Roasted Green Beans

Preheat oven to 450 degrees. Toss green beans in a shallow roasting pan with garlic, thyme and olive oil. Season with salt and pepper. Spread beans in a single layer and roast, turning occasionally until tender and lightly browned, 10 to 15 minutes. Discard thyme sprigs. Transfer beans to a serving bowl. Toss with lemon juice and lemon zest until well coated. Serve warm or at room temperature.

- 1 pound fresh green beans, trim stem ends only
- 3 cloves garlic, minced
- 3 fresh thyme sprigs, cut into thirds
- ¼ cup extra virgin olive oil
- Salt and freshly ground pepper, to taste
- 3 teaspoons fresh lemon juice
- Grated zest of 1 lemon

SERVINGS
8

# Green Beans with New Potatoes

Boil potatoes until fork tender, about 30 minutes. Drain. Boil beans until crisp tender, 8 to 10 minutes. Drain and rinse in cold water. In a small bowl whisk together remaining ingredients until well blended. Pour over potatoes and beans and serve warm.

- 2 pounds small red potatoes, unpeeled
- 1 pound fresh green beans, trimmed
- ½ cup vegetable oil
- 3 tablespoons white or red wine vinegar
- 2 tablespoons minced fresh basil or tarragon
- 1 teaspoon Dijon mustard
- 1 clove garlic, minced
- ¼ teaspoon granulated sugar
- Salt and freshly ground pepper, to taste

SERVINGS
4-6

# Broccoli Dijon

Cut broccoli into flowerets. Peel stalks and slice into ½-inch pieces. Sauté broccoli in oil until crisp tender. Whisk mustard and tarragon into vinegar and pour over broccoli. Season to taste and toss with walnuts.

1 pound fresh broccoli
¼ cup vegetable oil
1 teaspoon Dijon mustard
½ teaspoon dried tarragon
2 tablespoons white wine vinegar
Salt and freshly ground pepper, to taste
¼ cup chopped walnuts, toasted

SERVINGS
6-8

# Broccoli Soufflé

Preheat oven to 350 degrees. Butter a 2-quart soufflé dish. Purée broccoli, milk, salt, pepper, nutmeg, butter, flour, egg yolks and hot pepper sauce in a food processor until smooth. Pour into saucepan and cook over medium low heat until thickened, stirring constantly for 6 to 8 minutes. Allow mixture to cool. In a separate bowl beat egg whites until stiff but not dry. Carefully fold broccoli mixture and cheese into egg whites. Pour into prepared dish and bake until browned and puffed, 35 to 40 minutes. Serve immediately.

1 pound fresh broccoli, cooked
1½ cups warm milk
1 teaspoon salt
¼ teaspoon black pepper
⅛ teaspoon ground nutmeg
¼ cup butter, softened
3 tablespoons all-purpose flour
6 large eggs, separated
2 dashes hot pepper sauce
¼ cup freshly grated Parmesan cheese

SERVINGS
4-6

# WILTED CABBAGE

Cook bacon until crisp. Drain, reserving ¼ cup drippings, crumble and set aside. Add cabbage, onion, salt and nutmeg to reserved drippings. Cover and cook over low heat, stirring often until cabbage is wilted, 25 minutes. Whisk vinegar, sugar and red pepper until blended. Pour over cabbage and cook for 5 minutes. Toss with crumbled bacon.

4 slices bacon
5 cups coarsely chopped cabbage
1 medium onion, diced
1½ teaspoons salt
Pinch of ground nutmeg
2 tablespoons vinegar
1½ teaspoons granulated sugar
Pinch of ground red pepper

SERVINGS
6

# BRAISED CARROTS IN DILLED CREAM

Melt butter in a skillet and stir in sugar, salt and white pepper. Add carrots and sauté for 2 minutes, then stir in chicken broth. Place thyme under carrots, cover and simmer until carrots are tender, about 5 minutes. Uncover, increase heat to medium and reduce liquid until it glazes bottom of pan. Add crème fraîche and stir occasionally until thickened and carrots are coated. Remove sprig of thyme and stir in dill.

3 tablespoons unsalted butter
½ teaspoon granulated sugar
⅛ teaspoon salt
Freshly ground white pepper, to taste
8 to 10 medium carrots, julienned
3 tablespoons chicken broth
Sprig of fresh thyme or pinch of dried thyme
¾ cup crème fraîche (Page 61)
3 tablespoons fresh snipped dill

SERVINGS
6

# Orange Glazed Carrots

Combine all ingredients except carrots in a saucepan. Cook over medium heat until sugar is dissolved, stirring constantly. Add carrots, reduce heat and simmer until carrots are glazed, 15 minutes.

¼ cup butter
¼ cup granulated sugar
Grated zest and juice of
  1 small orange
¼ teaspoon ground ginger
  (optional)
12 carrots, peeled, sliced
  and cooked

It's hard to imagine
a civilization
without onions.

*Julia Child*

SERVINGS
6

# CAULIFLOWER PANACHE

Preheat oven to 350 degrees. Cut cauliflower into flowerets and cook until tender. Drain and place in a 1½-quart casserole dish. Cut broccoli into large pieces and cook until tender. Drain. In food processor purée broccoli with 2 tablespoons butter and sour cream. Season with salt and pepper. Sprinkle cauliflower with cheese and cover with broccoli purée. Sauté bread crumbs in 2 tablespoons melted butter until lightly toasted. Sprinkle on top of casserole. Bake for 20 minutes.

- 1 head cauliflower
- 1 pound fresh broccoli, stalks peeled
- ¼ cup butter, divided
- ½ cup sour cream
- Salt and freshly ground pepper, to taste
- ½ cup freshly grated Parmesan cheese
- ½ cup dry bread crumbs

SERVINGS
4-6

# SANTA FE SAUTÉ

Sauté bell peppers and garlic in oil over medium heat until tender. Stir in remaining ingredients and cook until thoroughly heated.

- ½ red bell pepper, diced
- ½ green bell pepper, diced
- 2 cloves garlic, minced
- 3 tablespoons vegetable oil
- 1½ cups fresh corn, cooked
- 2 tomatoes, peeled, seeded and diced
- 3 tablespoons red wine vinegar
- 2 tablespoons minced fresh cilantro
- 1 teaspoon ground cumin
- ½ teaspoon salt
- ⅛ teaspoon ground red pepper

SERVINGS
10

# Taos Corn Bake

Preheat oven to 350 degrees. Grease a 12 x 8-inch baking dish. Stir together sour cream, cheese and cilantro and set aside. Sauté onion and bell peppers in butter until tender. Add both cans of corn. In a separate bowl combine corn bread mix with eggs. Stir in corn mixture and spread in prepared dish. Spoon sour cream mixture randomly over top. Bake until golden brown, 50 to 60 minutes.

1 cup sour cream
1 cup (4 ounces) grated cheddar cheese
1 tablespoon minced fresh cilantro (optional)
1 small onion, diced
½ green bell pepper, diced
½ red bell pepper, diced
½ cup butter
1 can (15 ounces) whole kernel corn, with liquid
1 can (15 ounces) cream style corn
1 box (7½ ounces) corn bread mix
3 eggs, lightly beaten

SERVINGS
8

# Braised Fennel

Trim tops off fennel then cut each bulb in half lengthwise. Melt butter in a large skillet and stir in sugar until dissolved. Add garlic and sauté for 2 minutes. Place fennel in skillet, cut side down, cooking until well browned, 5 to 10 minutes. Turn fennel and add orange juice, water, salt and pepper. Bring to a boil, reduce heat and cover. Simmer until fennel is fork tender, 20 to 30 minutes. (If pan becomes dry during cooking, add a little more water.) Continue to cook uncovered at medium heat until liquid evaporates. Toss with parsley and serve immediately.

4 medium fennel bulbs
1½ tablespoons unsalted butter
1 teaspoon granulated sugar
2 cloves garlic, thinly sliced
¼ cup fresh orange juice
1 cup water
Salt and freshly ground pepper, to taste
½ cup fresh parsley leaves

SERVINGS
8

# PEAS, PEAS, PEAS

Boil sugar snap peas in 2 quarts water for 1 minute. Add snow peas, boil for 2 minutes and drain. Plunge immediately into ice water to stop cooking process. Stir in baby peas. Melt butter in a large skillet, add orange zest and juice and bring to a boil. Add peas, sauté until thoroughly heated and stir in salt.

- ½ pound fresh sugar snap peas, strings removed
- ½ pound fresh snow peas, strings removed
- 1 cup frozen baby peas, thawed
- 3 tablespoons butter
- Grated zest and juice of ½ orange
- ¼ teaspoon salt

SERVINGS
4-6

# SWEET & SAVORY PEPPER SAUTÉ

Pour water over raisins and let stand for 15 minutes. Sauté garlic in butter and oil for 1 minute. Add bell peppers and sauté for 1 minute. Stir in capers, olives and raisins with water. Cook covered for 2 minutes. Add pine nuts and toss.

- 2 tablespoons golden raisins
- ¼ cup boiling water
- 2 cloves garlic, thinly sliced
- 1 tablespoon unsalted butter
- 1 tablespoon olive oil
- 1 red bell pepper, julienned
- 1 yellow bell pepper, julienned
- 1 orange bell pepper, julienned
- 2 teaspoons capers, drained and coarsely chopped
- 4 kalamata or other brine-cured olives, thinly sliced
- 2 tablespoons pine nuts, toasted

SERVINGS 16

# Twice Baked Garlic Potatoes

Preheat oven to 400 degrees. Cut off and discard top of garlic. Place garlic on piece of foil, drizzle with olive oil and wrap tightly. Bake potatoes and garlic for 1 hour. Cut potatoes in half lengthwise, scoop out into a bowl and reserve shells. Unwrap garlic and squeeze cloves into potatoes. Mash potatoes and garlic with butter and enough milk to moisten. Blend in cream cheese, parsley, onions and salt. Spoon mixture back into potato shells. Sprinkle with cheese and paprika. Bake until cheese melts, 25 minutes.

1 head garlic
1 tablespoon olive oil
8 baking potatoes
½ cup butter
Milk
2 packages (3 ounces each) cream cheese, softened
¼ cup minced fresh parsley
¼ cup thinly sliced green onions
1 teaspoon salt
2 cups (8 ounces) grated cheddar cheese
Paprika

If this was adulthood, the only improvement she could detect in her situation was that now she could eat dessert without eating her vegetables.

*Lisa Alther*

SERVINGS
8

# Potato Gratin with Boursin

Preheat oven to 400 degrees. Butter a 13 x 9-inch casserole dish. In a food processor combine cream and Boursin cheese until smooth. Arrange half of the potatoes in baking dish in slightly overlapping rows. Season with salt and pepper. Spoon one-half cheese mixture over potatoes. Arrange remaining potatoes in dish and season with salt and pepper. Spoon remaining cheese mixture over casserole. Bake until potatoes are golden brown, 1 hour. Sprinkle with parsley before serving.

- 2 cups heavy cream
- 1 package (5 ounces) Boursin cheese with herbs
- 3 pounds small red potatoes, unpeeled and thinly sliced
- Salt and freshly ground pepper, to taste
- 1½ tablespoons minced fresh parsley

*Boursin mixture (page 36) may be substituted for Boursin cheese.*

SERVINGS
8

# Lemon Parsley Potatoes

Cover potatoes, lemon and onion with salted water. Boil until potatoes are fork tender, about 20 minutes. Drain, discarding lemon and onion. Melt butter in a small saucepan and stir in lemon juice, zest, salt and pepper. Pour over potatoes and toss with parsley.

- 3 pounds small red potatoes, unpeeled and cut into quarters
- 1 lemon, cut into quarters
- 1 medium onion, cut into quarters
- ½ cup butter
- 1 teaspoon fresh lemon juice
- 2 teaspoons grated lemon zest
- ½ teaspoon salt
- ⅛ teaspoon black pepper
- ½ cup minced fresh parsley

SERVINGS 8

# O'KEEFFE'S POTATOES

Cover potatoes with salted water and bring to a boil. Cook until fork tender, about 25 minutes. Drain. Cover cabbage with water and bring to a boil. Cook until fork tender, 5 to 7 minutes. Drain and set aside. Mash potatoes with milk, butter, salt and pepper. Stir in cabbage and onions.

6 medium potatoes, peeled and cut into eighths
3 cups coarsely shredded cabbage
¾ cup milk
¼ cup butter
1 teaspoon salt
½ teaspoon black pepper
2 green onions, thinly sliced

SERVINGS 8

# MASHED POTATOES WITH TURNIPS

Preheat oven to 350 degrees. Butter a 2-quart casserole dish. Peel potatoes, turnip and onion and cut into 1-inch pieces. In a Dutch oven cover vegetables with salted water and bring to a boil. Reduce heat and simmer until fork tender, about 30 minutes. Drain and mash vegetables with butter and enough milk to moisten. Stir in cream cheese, sour cream and horseradish. Season with salt and pepper. Spread in prepared dish and bake for 20 minutes.

4 large potatoes
1 medium turnip
1 medium onion
2 tablespoons butter, softened
Milk
1 package (3 ounces) cream cheese, softened
½ cup sour cream
1½ teaspoons horseradish (optional)
Salt and freshly ground pepper, to taste

SERVINGS
6

# SOPHISTICATED SPINACH

Preheat oven to 325 degrees. Butter a 13 x 9-inch baking dish. Cook spinach according to package directions. Drain and squeeze dry. Melt 2 tablespoons butter in a skillet and sauté mushrooms until tender. Remove from heat and stir in spinach, mayonnaise, sour cream, cheese, salt and pepper. Spoon mixture into artichoke bottoms and place in prepared dish. Melt remaining butter in a small saucepan and sauté bread crumbs until lightly toasted. Sprinkle artichoke bottoms with bread crumbs and tomato. Bake for 20 minutes.

1 package (10 ounces) frozen chopped spinach
¼ cup butter, divided
¼ pound fresh mushrooms, sliced
2 tablespoons mayonnaise
2 tablespoons sour cream
2 tablespoons freshly grated Parmesan cheese
½ teaspoon salt
¼ teaspoon black pepper
2 cans (14 ounces each) artichoke bottoms, drained
½ cup dry bread crumbs
1 plum tomato, seeded and diced

8

# GRILLED SQUASH

Cut zucchini and squash diagonally into ½-inch slices. Sprinkle with salt and wrap in paper towel for 30 minutes. Pat dry, place in shallow dish or zippered plastic bag and cover with marinade. Grill over low coals, basting occasionally with marinade until vegetables are light brown and fork tender, about 15 minutes.

Vegetable Marinade: Whisk all marinade ingredients until well blended.

*An excellent marinade for all grilled vegetables.*

4 medium zucchini
4 medium yellow squash
Salt
VEGETABLE MARINADE:
¼ cup olive oil
6 tablespoons fresh lemon juice
1 tablespoon Dijon mustard
1 teaspoon salt
1 teaspoon freshly ground pepper
2 cloves garlic, minced

SERVINGS
6

# Spaghetti Squash with Two Cheeses

- 1 spaghetti squash
- 2 cloves garlic
- 1 cup (4 ounces) grated cheddar cheese
- 1 cup tomato sauce
- 2 tablespoons minced fresh basil
- ½ teaspoon salt
- ¼ teaspoon black pepper
- 2 tablespoons freshly grated Parmesan cheese

Preheat oven to 350 degrees. Halve squash lengthwise, remove and discard seeds. In a Dutch oven cover squash with water, add 1 whole clove garlic and boil until squash strands loosen easily, 30 minutes. Drain and discard garlic. Cool squash cut side down for 20 minutes. Carefully scoop squash from shells into a large bowl. Stir in 1 minced clove garlic, cheddar cheese, tomato sauce, basil, salt and pepper. Spoon mixture back into squash shells or spread into a buttered casserole dish. Sprinkle with Parmesan cheese and bake for 20 minutes.

If you can keep your head when all about you are losing theirs, it's just possible you haven't grasped the situation.

*Jean Kerr*

SERVINGS 8

# ALMOND STUFFED ZUCCHINI

Preheat oven to 350 degrees. Grease a 13 x 9-inch baking dish. Cook zucchini until just tender. Cool slightly. Scoop zucchini from shells, taking care to leave skins intact. Chop zucchini and reserve to use in stuffing. Place shells in prepared dish. In a saucepan over medium heat, sauté onion and bell pepper in oil until tender, 5 to 7 minutes. Stir in garlic and cook for 2 minutes. Remove from heat and stir in reserved zucchini, thyme and almonds. Season with salt and pepper. Spoon filling into shells. Bake until thoroughly heated, 15 minutes.

**4 medium zucchini, cut in half lengthwise**
**1 medium onion, diced**
**2 red bell peppers, diced**
**2 tablespoons olive oil**
**2 cloves garlic, minced**
**2 teaspoons minced fresh thyme**
**6 tablespoons sliced almonds, toasted**
**Salt and freshly ground pepper, to taste**

SERVINGS 6

# ZUCCHINI AU GRATIN

Preheat oven to 350 degrees. Butter a deep 2-quart casserole dish. Sauté onion in 2 tablespoons butter until tender. In prepared dish layer one-half the zucchini, onion, tomatoes and mozzarella cheese. Dot with 2 tablespoons butter and season with salt and pepper. Repeat layers. Combine bread crumbs with Parmesan cheese and sprinkle on top. Bake uncovered for 45 minutes. (If casserole becomes dry during baking, add 2 tablespoons water.)

**½ cup diced onion**
**6 tablespoons butter, divided**
**3 cups sliced zucchini**
**3 small tomatoes, peeled and diced**
**2 cups (8 ounces) grated mozzarella cheese**
**Salt and freshly ground pepper, to taste**
**⅓ cup dry Italian bread crumbs**
**⅓ cup freshly grated Parmesan cheese**

SERVINGS
8

# FRESH TOMATO TART

Crust for 9-inch pie
4 or 5 tomatoes, peeled
1 teaspoon salt
2 tablespoons fresh minced basil
4 green onions, thinly sliced
Freshly ground pepper, to taste
2 tablespoons freshly grated Parmesan cheese
2 tablespoons dry bread crumbs
1 tablespoon butter, cut into small pieces

Preheat oven to 450 degrees. Line a 9-inch tart pan with pie crust. Prick bottom and sides with a fork. Bake for 10 to 12 minutes or until golden. Set aside to cool.

Cut tomatoes into ½-inch slices and place on paper towels. Sprinkle with ½ teaspoon salt and let stand for 30 minutes. Turn over onto fresh paper towels, sprinkle with ½ teaspoon salt and let stand for 30 more minutes.

Preheat oven to 350 degrees. Arrange tomatoes in tart shell. Sprinkle basil and onions over tomatoes and season with pepper. Combine cheese with bread crumbs and sprinkle over top. Dot with butter and bake on upper rack for 30 minutes. Cool for 5 minutes before cutting.

SERVINGS
6

# HERBED CHERRY TOMATOES

2 shallots, minced
4 green onions, thinly sliced
2 tablespoons minced fresh parsley
1 teaspoon dried dill weed
¼ cup butter
3 cups cherry tomatoes
½ teaspoon salt

Sauté shallots, onions, parsley and dill in butter until tender. Add tomatoes and salt. Cook, stirring gently until a few tomato skins burst, 5 to 7 minutes. Tomatoes should be well coated with butter-herb mixture.

SERVINGS
10

# Vegetable Terrine

8 ounces feta cheese
4 ounces cream cheese, softened
4 eggs
¼ teaspoon white pepper
¼ teaspoon ground nutmeg
1 teaspoon lemon juice
10 ounces fresh spinach, stems removed
1 bunch green onions, thinly sliced
½ cup butter, divided
2 large red bell peppers, diced
8 ounces fresh mushrooms, sliced
6 sheets frozen phyllo dough, thawed

Butter a 9 x 5 x 3-inch loaf pan and line completely with a double thickness of foil, leaving 1 inch excess on sides to serve as handles when removing terrine. Butter foil. In a mixing bowl beat feta cheese, cream cheese, eggs, white pepper, nutmeg and lemon juice until smooth. Set aside.

Microwave spinach until wilted, 3 minutes. Cool and squeeze dry. In a skillet sauté onions and spinach in 1 tablespoon butter for 3 minutes. Stir in one-third of cheese mixture. Remove from skillet and set aside.

In same skillet melt 1 tablespoon butter and sauté red peppers until tender, 3 to 5 minutes. Stir in one-third of cheese mixture. Remove from skillet and set aside.

In same skillet melt 1 tablespoon butter and sauté mushrooms until tender, 5 to 7 minutes. Stir in remaining cheese mixture. Remove from skillet and set aside.

Preheat oven to 350 degrees. Melt remaining 5 tablespoons of butter in a small saucepan. Cut phyllo dough in half to make 12 sheets (8 x 12 inches). Cover with plastic wrap. Remove 4 sheets. Brush each sheet lightly with melted butter and stack one on top of the other. Place in bottom and up over sides of pan. Remove 2 more sheets, brush with butter and place in bottom of pan. Cover with spinach mixture and fold over to enclose. Butter two more sheets and place on top of spinach packet. Cover with red pepper mixture and fold over to enclose. Repeat with two more sheets and mushroom mixture. Brush remaining two sheets of phyllo with butter and fold into thirds to fit on top of pan. Cover with phyllo that extends over sides of pan. (May be prepared one day ahead up to this point.) Bake until top is brown and puffy, 1 hour. Let stand for 10 minutes, remove from pan and slice.

SERVINGS
Allow 4 to 6 pieces per person

# OVEN ROASTED VEGETABLES

Extra virgin olive oil
Sea salt
Freshly ground pepper

Preheat oven to 400 degrees. Select a variety of vegetables in desired amounts. Prepare vegetables and arrange on baking sheets or in a roasting pan. Brush generously with olive oil (about 2 tablespoons per 1½ pounds of vegetables). Sprinkle with salt and pepper. Roast vegetables that take longest to cook first, adding other vegetables at appropriate times. Test for tenderness by piercing with a fork. If some vegetables are done before others, remove them from oven and set aside. Serve hot or at room temperature.

40 to 45 minutes cooking time:
Potatoes cut into wedges or small red potatoes, whole
Carrots, peeled and cut into halves
Winter squash, peeled, seeded and cut into wedges
Sweet potatoes, peeled and cut into wedges.

25 to 30 minutes cooking time:
Eggplant, cut into 1-inch slices
Onions, cut into quarters
Sweet corn, ears cut into halves
Small beets, peeled

15 to 20 minutes cooking time:
Asparagus spears, tough ends removed
Green beans, trimmed
Zucchini, cut into quarters
Yellow squash, cut into quarters
Bell peppers, cut into quarters or sixths

**If you obey all the rules, you miss all the fun.**

*Katherine Hepburn*

SERVINGS 20

# Marinated Vegetables

In a Dutch oven bring 2 inches of water to a boil. Add cauliflower and carrots, reduce heat and simmer for 5 minutes. Add green beans, asparagus and peas. Continue to simmer until vegetables are crisp tender, 5 minutes. Drain and immediately rinse in cold water. Gently stir in artichokes, bell pepper and olives. Pour marinade over vegetables. Cover and chill for at least 12 hours, tossing occasionally. Line a large, deep platter with radicchio leaves. Drain vegetables and arrange on platter.

Marinade: Wisk together all ingredients.

1 medium head cauliflower, cut into flowerets
1 pound carrots, peeled and cut diagonally into ½-inch pieces
1 pound fresh green beans, trimmed
½ pound fresh asparagus spears, cut diagonally into 2-inch pieces
1 cup fresh snow peas or sugar snap peas, strings removed
1 can (14 ounces) artichoke hearts, drained and cut into quarters
1 red bell pepper, sliced
1 can (5¾ ounces) pitted black olives, drained
Radicchio or red cabbage leaves
MARINADE:
1¼ cups vegetable oil
1 cup tarragon vinegar
5 teaspoons salt
1 teaspoon granulated sugar
¾ teaspoon crushed red pepper

SERVINGS 8

# Baked Ratatouille

Preheat oven to 300 degrees. Place eggplant in a deep 3-quart baking dish. Add garlic, then layers of onion, bell peppers, zucchini and tomatoes. Season with salt and pepper. Pour tomato juice over top. Press vegetables with back of a large spoon to make ratatouille more compact. Combine basil and olive oil. Drizzle over top. Place casserole in oven and reduce heat to 275 degrees. Bake uncovered for 3 hours. Serve hot or cold.

1 eggplant, peeled and diced
1 clove garlic, minced
1 large onion, thinly sliced
1 large green bell pepper, diced
1 large red bell pepper, diced
1 zucchini, sliced
4 tomatoes, peeled and diced
Salt and freshly ground pepper, to taste
1 cup tomato juice
¼ cup minced fresh basil
¼ cup olive oil

SERVINGS
10

# Winter Vegetable Couscous

Layer cabbage, onion, turnips, sweet potato and carrots in a 2-quart microwave dish. Drizzle with water and olive oil. Cover and microwave on high for 10 minutes. Stir vegetables, cover and microwave on high until vegetables are fork tender, 5 to 7 minutes.

Combine tomatoes with cumin, coriander, ½ teaspoon turmeric and salt. Stir mixture into vegetables. Add garbanzo beans, cover and microwave on high for 3 minutes. Set aside. Combine water, ½ teaspoon turmeric, ginger and cinnamon in a 4-cup glass measure. Cover with vented plastic wrap and microwave on high for 6 minutes or until mixture boils. Stir in couscous. Cover and microwave on high for 2 minutes. Let stand until moisture is absorbed, 5 minutes. Serve vegetables over couscous and top with almonds and raisins.

**2 cups coarsely chopped cabbage**
**1 medium onion, diced**
**2 medium turnips or white potatoes, peeled and cubed**
**1 sweet potato or butternut squash, peeled and cubed**
**2 carrots or parsnips, peeled and sliced**
**¼ cup water**
**2 tablespoons olive oil**
**1 can (14½ ounces) diced tomatoes, with liquid**
**½ teaspoon ground cumin**
**½ teaspoon ground coriander**
**1 teaspoon ground turmeric, divided**
**½ teaspoon salt**
**1 can (15 ounces) garbanzo beans, drained**
**2 cups water**
**¼ teaspoon ground ginger**
**¼ teaspoon ground cinnamon**
**1 cup couscous or white rice**
**½ cup slivered almonds, toasted**
**⅓ cup raisins**

SERVINGS 10

# LEBANESE LENTILS

Cover lentils with water, add salt and cook for 20 minutes. Stir in rice and cook for 20 minutes. Sauté onions in oil over medium heat until golden brown. Drain oil from onions into lentils and rice and set onions aside. Continue cooking lentils and rice until moisture is absorbed. To serve, arrange lentils on a platter and spoon onions over top. Individual servings of Lebanese Lentils are traditionally topped with Salata (page 63).

**1 cup lentils**
**6 cups water**
**2 teaspoons salt**
**¾ cup long-grain white rice**
**3 large onions, slivered**
**½ cup olive oil**

SERVINGS 8

# GOOD LUCK PEAS

Combine all ingredients in a large saucepan. Cover and simmer for 1 hour over low heat, stirring occasionally.

*Black-eyed peas are traditionally eaten on New Year's Day for a year of good luck.*

**2 cans (16 ounces each) black-eyed peas, with liquid**
**3½ ounces pepperoni, diced**
**1 medium green bell pepper, diced**
**1 medium onion, diced**
**2 tablespoons picante sauce**
**¼ teaspoon hot pepper sauce**
**Salt, to taste**

SERVINGS
16

# FIVE BEAN BAKE

Preheat oven to 300 degrees. Cook bacon until crisp. Drain, reserving 2 tablespoons drippings, crumble and set aside. Sauté onion in drippings until tender, 5 to 8 minutes. Drain well. In a 3½-quart casserole dish combine all ingredients, stirring in brandy last. Bake uncovered for 2 hours.

- 6 slices bacon
- 1 medium onion, diced
- 1 cup ketchup
- ½ cup packed brown sugar
- 2 teaspoons Worcestershire sauce
- 1 tablespoon dry mustard
- 1 can (16 ounces) green beans, drained
- 1 can (16 ounces) wax beans, drained
- 1 can (16 ounces) kidney beans, rinsed and drained
- 1 can (15 ounces) pork and beans
- 1 can (16 ounces) garbanzo beans, drained
- ¼ cup brandy

**Experience is what you get looking for something else.**

*Mary Pettibone Poole*

SERVINGS 8

# HURRY UP BEANS

In a medium skillet cook bacon until crisp. Drain, reserving 2 tablespoons drippings, crumble and set aside. Sauté onion in reserved drippings until tender. Stir in bacon, picante sauce, ketchup, brown sugar and cumin. Add beans and bring to a boil. Reduce heat and simmer uncovered until thickened, 20 minutes.

4 slices bacon
½ cup diced onion
⅓ cup picante sauce
2 tablespoons ketchup
2 tablespoons packed brown sugar
½ teaspoon ground cumin
2 cans (16 ounces each) pork and beans

SERVINGS 4-6

# BUTTERNUT RISOTTO

Cut squash into eighths, discarding seeds. Steam until fork tender. Scoop squash from skin and lightly mash. Melt 1 tablespoon butter in saucepan, add oil and sauté shallots for 2 minutes. Add rice and cook for 5 minutes, stirring often. Add wine and continue cooking until liquid is nearly absorbed. Add squash and 1 cup heated chicken broth. Simmer until liquid is nearly absorbed. Continue stirring in broth one ladle at a time until rice is creamy and firm, 15 to 20 minutes. Season with nutmeg, salt and pepper. Stir in rosemary, remaining butter and ¼ cup cheese. Serve in shallow bowls garnished with remaining cheese and rosemary sprigs.

1 medium butternut squash
2 tablespoons unsalted butter, divided
1 tablespoon olive oil
4 shallots, minced
2 cups Arborio rice
½ cup dry white wine
5 to 6 cups chicken broth, heated
Freshly grated nutmeg, to taste
Salt and freshly ground pepper, to taste
1 tablespoon minced fresh rosemary
½ cup freshly grated Parmesan cheese, divided
Rosemary sprigs for garnish

SERVINGS
10-12

# PISTACHIO DRESSING

Preheat oven to 350 degrees. Lightly grease a 2-quart casserole dish. In a large saucepan bring chicken broth to a boil and add rice. Cover and cook until liquid is absorbed, 35 minutes. Sauté onions in butter until tender. Add sausage, crumble and brown. Drain well. Combine sausage, rice, parsley, sage, salt and pepper. Stir in pistachio nuts, butter and wine. Bake in prepared dish for 35 minutes.

**3½ cups chicken broth**
**1½ cups brown rice or wild rice**
**¾ cup thinly sliced green onions**
**¼ cup butter**
**½ cup bulk sausage, crumbled**
**¼ cup minced fresh parsley**
**½ teaspoon ground sage**
**Salt and freshly ground pepper, to taste**
**¾ cup pistachio nuts, coarsely chopped**
**¼ cup butter, melted**
**¼ cup dry white wine or vermouth**

SERVINGS
8-10

# CITRUS RICE

Sauté rice, lemon zest and garlic in butter until rice is opaque, about 5 minutes. Add to chicken broth, cover and simmer until liquid is absorbed, 20 minutes. Remove garlic and discard. Stir in lemon juice. Slowly stir in cream, onions and parsley. Continue to cook rice over low heat, stirring constantly until cream is absorbed, about 5 minutes. Season with salt and pepper.

**2 cups long-grain white rice**
**Grated zest of 2 lemons**
**1 clove garlic**
**½ cup butter**
**3½ cups boiling chicken broth**
**2 tablespoons fresh lemon juice**
**½ cup heavy cream**
**2 green onions, thinly sliced**
**¼ cup minced fresh parsley**
**Salt and freshly ground pepper, to taste**

SERVINGS
6

# VERMICELLI PILAF

Soak rice in water for 15 minutes, then drain. In a large saucepan brown uncooked vermicelli in olive oil for 5 to 7 minutes. Add rice and continue to cook for 2 minutes. Bring water and salt to a boil. Pour over vermicelli mixture and return to a boil. Cover, reduce heat and simmer for 20 minutes. Remove from heat and let stand for 5 minutes. Stir before serving.

**2 cups long-grain white rice**
**3/4 cup coiled vermicelli, broken into 1/2-inch pieces**
**2 tablespoons olive oil**
**3 cups water**
**1 tablespoon salt**

SERVINGS
8

# WILD RICE PILAF

Sauté celery, onions and mushrooms in butter in a large saucepan until tender. Add wild rice and sauté for 3 minutes. Add chicken broth, salt and pepper and bring to a boil. Reduce heat, cover and simmer until rice is tender, 45 minutes. Drain and toss with pecans.

**1 cup diced celery**
**1 cup diced onion**
**1/2 pound fresh mushrooms, sliced**
**1/4 cup butter**
**8 ounces wild rice**
**1 can (14 1/2 ounces) chicken broth**
**1/2 teaspoon salt**
**1/2 teaspoon black pepper**
**1/3 cup chopped pecans, toasted**

SERVINGS 6

# FRUITED WILD RICE PILAF

4 cups chicken broth
1 cup wild rice
¾ cup dried cherries
1 tablespoon butter
Grated zest and juice of 1 orange
½ cup chopped pecans, toasted
Salt and freshly ground pepper, to taste

Bring chicken broth and wild rice to a boil. Reduce heat, cover and simmer until rice is tender, 45 minutes. Add cherries and continue cooking for 5 minutes. Drain. Stir in butter, orange zest, juice, pecans, salt and pepper.

When I'm old and gray,
I want a house by the sea.
And a damn good
kitchen to cook in.

*Ava Gardner*

# LET THEM EAT CAKE

## "If we knew you were comin', we'd a-baked a gâteau."

Marie Antoinette was the queen of impeccable taste. But most of her taste was located in her sweet tooth, which legend says was as big as the Eiffel Tower. ❖ And, perhaps even more unfortunate for France, and ultimately for Marie, it was not a commoner's sweet tooth. No humble HoHo cakes for her Highness. No bourgeois Bama Pie snacks. ***Mais non***! Marie's passion for high-dollar sweets, flavored with apple honey from Normandy, citrus from Spain and vanilla beans from the tropics drove more than one pastry chef into a babbling fit. But that wasn't the worst fate that could befall a royal cook. Serve Marie a less-than-perfect pastry and her minions would drive Chef Jean Pierre to the guillotine. (An instrument designed initially to slice the huge jellyrolls of which Marie was so fond.) ❖ Finally, as with any addiction, Marie's sugar fetish got out of hand. She called for a competition from the great *pâtissieres* of France. "Bake!" she cried. "Bake, and the best may keep their heads." ❖ And so the bakers began to mix and whip, fold and form, concocting gigantic confections. Marie could not taste them fast enough and her servants began to stack the extras in the anterooms. ❖ Speaking of stacking up, so was the crowd outside the palace. Peasants who had been on rations of bread and water (well, not much bread) for months were driven into a frenzy by the aromas emanating from the royal ovens. Hearing about the angry crowd, Marie told her maître d' to serve them the extra desserts. ❖ Bad mistake. Caught in the throes of a massive, collective sugar rush, the crowd stormed the palace, severely altered Marie's hat size and created democracy. ❖ The moral of the story is: desserts are good for you and good for society as well.

# Desserts

SERVINGS 8

# TRUFFLED PEARS

6 ounces high quality bittersweet chocolate
8 ripe D'anjou or Comice pears
1 package (16 ounces) puff pastry dough, thawed
1 egg
2 tablespoons milk
½ cup butter
¾ cup packed brown sugar
¼ cup heavy cream
2 tablespoons rum

Melt chocolate and stir until smooth. Cool until chocolate is firm enough to hold a shape. Using a melon scoop, make 8 chocolate balls. Set aside. Peel pears, leaving stem intact. If necessary, slice a thin piece off bottom of each pear so it will stand upright. Slice horizontally through each pear 1 inch from bottom. Remove seeds with melon scoop and replace with a chocolate ball. Replace top of pear.

Roll out puff pastry and cut into eight 6-inch squares. Cut a small triangle out of each side to form an "X" shape. Reserve triangles. Place each pear in center of an "X" and bring up sides to completely enclose pear. Pinch seams to close. Cut reserved triangles into leaf-shaped pieces. In a small bowl whisk together egg and milk. Brush pastry leaves with egg mixture and place 4 leaves on each pear over seams. Cover each tightly with plastic wrap and chill for 1 to 4 hours. Cover and chill remaining egg mixture.

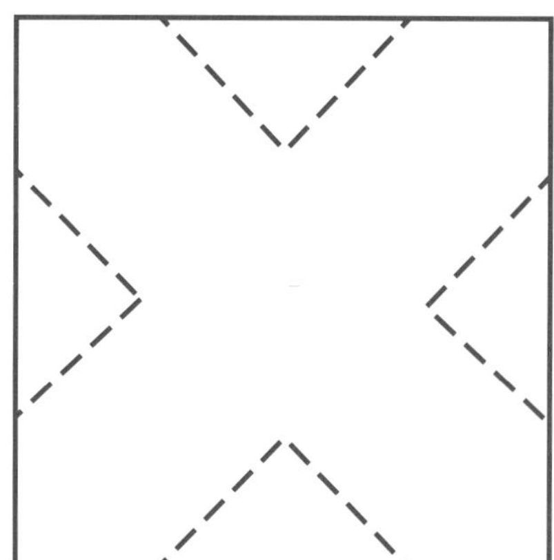

Preheat oven to 400 degrees. Line a baking sheet with parchment paper. Remove plastic wrap from pears and place on prepared pan. Brush pears with egg mixture and bake until golden brown, 20 minutes.

Melt butter, add brown sugar and boil for 1 minute. Remove from heat and stir in cream and rum. Spoon warm sauce onto dessert plates and place pear in center.

SERVINGS
12

# CHOCOLATE BOUCHÉES WITH CRÈME ANGLAISE

6 tablespoons butter
6 ounces bittersweet chocolate
3 large eggs, separated
$^{2}/_{3}$ cup granulated sugar, divided
1 teaspoon vanilla extract
12 spring roll wrappers (7 to 9-inch)

CRÈME ANGLAISE:
3 egg yolks, lightly beaten
$^{1}/_{3}$ cup granulated sugar
$1\,^{1}/_{4}$ cups hot milk
2 teaspoons vanilla extract
1 tablespoon butter

Preheat oven to 400 degrees. Butter a 12-count muffin pan. Melt butter and chocolate in microwave, stirring every 30 seconds. In a large bowl whisk egg yolks with $^{1}/_{3}$ cup sugar until smooth. Whisk in melted chocolate and vanilla. Beat egg whites in a large bowl until soft peaks form. Gradually beat in remaining sugar until stiff. Fold egg whites into chocolate mixture.

Place a spring roll wrapper in each muffin cup. Spoon $^{1}/_{3}$ cup chocolate mixture into each wrapper. Gather up corners and gently twist to form a pouch. (Bouchées may stand at room temperature for up to 2 hours before baking.) Bake until bouchées are browned on tips, 10 to 12 minutes. Cool for 5 minutes before removing from pan. Spoon crème anglaise on each serving plate and place bouchée in center.

Crème Anglaise: Whisk egg yolks and sugar in a medium saucepan until smooth. Whisk in milk 1 tablespoon at a time. Cook over low heat, stirring constantly until mixture is thick enough to coat the back of a spoon. Do not allow mixture to boil. Remove from heat and stir in vanilla and butter. Crème anglaise may be made ahead and refrigerated. Warm over low heat before serving.

**Research tells us that fourteen out of ten individuals like chocolate.**

*Sandra Boynton*

SERVINGS
10

# ALMOND CHOCOLATE TORTE

Preheat oven to 350 degrees. Grease a 15½ x 10½ x 1-inch jelly-roll pan. Line pan with waxed paper and generously grease again. Beat egg whites with salt in a large bowl until soft peaks form. Beat in 1 cup sugar two tablespoons at a time. Fold in cocoa. In a separate bowl beat egg yolks until lemon-colored. Fold egg yolks and vanilla into cocoa mixture. Spread in prepared pan and bake until cake springs back when gently pressed with fingertip, 20 minutes. Remove from oven and invert onto a tea towel dusted with confectioners' sugar. Carefully lift pan and immediately remove paper. Cool then cut crosswise into fourths.

Whip cream until it starts to thicken. Add sugar and vanilla and beat until thick enough to hold firm peaks. Spread whipped cream evenly over three pieces of torte and place on top of one another on a serving platter. Top with remaining piece of torte. Spread glaze over top, allowing it to drizzle down the sides. Sprinkle with almonds. Chill until ready to serve.

Glaze: Melt chocolate and butter in a small saucepan over low heat. Add sugar, water, vanilla and salt. Beat until smooth and glossy.

5 large eggs, separated
¼ teaspoon salt
1 cup confectioners' sugar, sifted
¼ cup cocoa powder, sifted
1 teaspoon vanilla extract
1 cup heavy cream
¼ cup confectioners' sugar
1 teaspoon vanilla extract
⅓ cup sliced almonds, toasted
GLAZE:
1 ounce unsweetened chocolate
1 tablespoon butter
½ cup confectioners' sugar
2 tablespoons boiling water
½ teaspoon vanilla extract
Pinch of salt

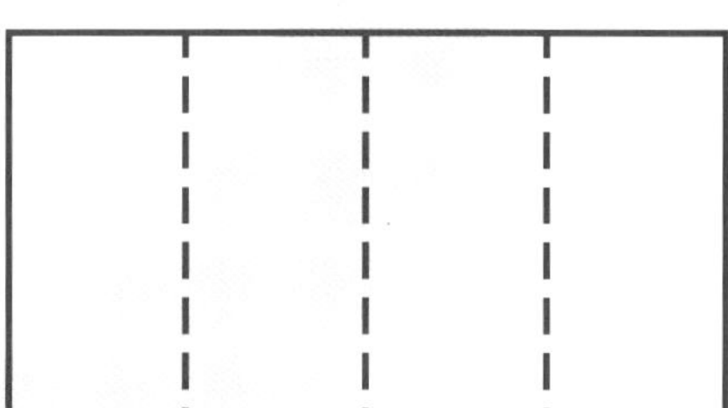

SERVINGS
8

# Strawberry Marzipan Torte

Torte: Preheat oven to 350 degrees. Combine all ingredients in a large bowl and blend well. Spread dough evenly in two ungreased 9-inch round pans.

Marzipan: Beat egg with electric mixer in a small bowl. Gradually add sugar and beat until thick. Blend in almond paste and extract at low speed. Divide and spread over torte batter and bake until light golden brown, 25 to 30 minutes. Cool for 5 minutes. Remove from pans then transfer to a wire rack to cool completely.

Filling: Whip cream until it starts to thicken. Add sugar and kirsch and beat until thick enough to hold firm peaks. Divide filling between two bowls. Place one torte layer on serving plate, marzipan side up. Slice half the strawberries and fold into half the filling. Spread over torte layer and top with second torte layer, marzipan side up. Spread remaining filling over torte and garnish with whole strawberries. Chill for several hours before serving.

**TORTE:**
**2 cups all-purpose flour**
**½ cup granulated sugar**
**¼ teaspoon salt**
**1 teaspoon vanilla extract**
**1 cup butter, softened**
**1 egg**
**MARZIPAN:**
**1 egg**
**¼ cup granulated sugar**
**½ cup almond paste**
**½ teaspoon almond extract**
**FILLING:**
**1 cup heavy cream**
**2 tablespoons confectioners' sugar**
**1 tablespoon kirsch liqueur**
**1 quart strawberries**

SERVINGS
16

# CHOCOLATE APRICOT TORTE

GARNISH:
4 ounces semisweet chocolate
1 tablespoon shortening (no substitute)
CAKE:
1¼ cups unsifted cake flour
⅔ cup cocoa powder
8 large egg yolks
1¾ cups + 1 tablespoon granulated sugar
¼ teaspoon salt
12 large egg whites
½ teaspoon salt
½ teaspoon cream of tartar
FILLING:
1 jar (12 ounces) apricot preserves
6 tablespoons amaretto liqueur
2 cups heavy cream
⅓ cup confectioners' sugar
1 cup sliced almonds, toasted

Press waxed paper into bottom of 10-inch springform pan. Microwave chocolate and shortening until melted. Pour into prepared pan and tilt to spread evenly. Chill until chocolate just begins to set, 15 to 20 minutes. Remove sides of pan. Using a ruler as a guide, cut 16 pie-shaped wedges with a sharp knife, wiping knife between cuts. Chill overnight.

Cake: Preheat oven to 325 degrees. Butter and flour a 10-inch springform pan. Sift together flour and cocoa. In a large bowl beat egg yolks, sugar and salt until thick and lemon-colored, about 2 minutes. Add ½ cup egg whites and blend. Slowly add flour mixture. (Batter will be very thick.) Beat remaining egg whites, salt and cream of tartar in a large bowl until stiff peaks form. Do not overbeat. Stir a third of the egg whites into cake batter. Fold in remaining egg whites. Carefully pour batter into prepared pan and bake until a wooden toothpick inserted in center comes out clean, 1¼ hours. Remove from oven and run a knife around edges of pan. Cool for 10 minutes, remove sides and transfer to a wire rack to cool completely. Slice evenly into 3 layers.

Filling: Combine preserves with enough amaretto to make a spreadable mixture. Set aside. Whip cream until it starts to thicken. Add sugar and remaining amaretto and beat until thick enough to hold firm peaks. Spread preserves evenly over two torte layers and top each with a thin layer of whipped cream. Place layers on top of one another on a serving platter. Top with remaining torte layer. Spread whipped cream smoothly around sides and top. Gently press almonds onto sides. Place chocolate wedges on edge on top of cake with points toward center. Place remaining whipped cream in pastry bag fitted with rosette tip and pipe a rosette in front of each chocolate wedge.

SERVINGS
8-10

# KIWI PAVLOVA

**MERINGUE:**
2 large egg whites
1½ cups superfine granulated sugar
1 teaspoon vanilla extract
1 teaspoon malt vinegar
¼ cup boiling water

**TOPPING:**
1 cup heavy cream
2 tablespoons granulated sugar
1 teaspoon vanilla extract
2 kiwi fruit, peeled and sliced

Preheat oven to 400 degrees. Line a baking sheet with heavy-duty foil and mark a 10-inch circle in center. Butter circle and set aside. Place all meringue ingredients in a large bowl, adding boiling water last. Beat for 30 minutes (yes, 30 minutes) on medium speed with an electric mixer. Spread meringue evenly on foil circle. Place baking sheet on bottom rack and turn heat off. Leave in oven for 2 hours with the door closed.

Topping: Whip cream until it starts to thicken. Add sugar and vanilla and beat until thick enough to hold firm peaks. Spread topping over meringue and garnish with kiwi fruit.

*Strawberries, sliced peaches or other seasonal fruits may be substituted as a garnish.*

Nobody's interested in Sweetness and light.

*Hedda Hopper*

SERVINGS
10-12

# MARIE'S MOCHA GÂTEAU

Preheat oven to 350 degrees. Line a 9-inch springform pan with foil and butter the bottom and sides. Melt chocolate, sugar and butter in microwave. Stir until smooth and cool slightly. Add coffee and beat in eggs. Pour batter into prepared pan and bake until a crust forms, 40 minutes. Cool in pan to room temperature, then chill overnight. Remove cake from pan, spread with topping and garnish with assorted berries.

Topping: Whip cream until it starts to thicken. Add sugar and vanilla and beat until thick enough to hold firm peaks.

**CAKE:**
**8 ounces quality semisweet chocolate**
**1 cup granulated sugar**
**1 cup butter**
**½ cup cold coffee**
**4 eggs**
**Assorted berries**
**TOPPING:**
**1 cup heavy cream**
**¼ cup confectioners' sugar**
**1 teaspoon vanilla extract**

SERVINGS
8

# ALMOND CAKE

Preheat oven to 350 degrees. Grease and flour a 9-inch round cake pan. Cream butter and sugar in a large bowl. Stir in almond paste, eggs and almond extract until smooth. Combine flour and baking powder and add to mixture, blending thoroughly. Pour into prepared pan and bake for 25 minutes. Cool for 10 minutes. Remove from pan and transfer to a wire rack to cool completely. Before serving, dust with confectioners' sugar. Garnish with fresh berries and grated chocolate.

**½ cup unsalted butter, softened**
**¾ cup granulated sugar**
**8 ounces almond paste**
**3 eggs**
**¼ teaspoon almond extract**
**¼ cup all-purpose flour**
**⅓ teaspoon baking powder**
**Confectioners' sugar**
**Fresh berries**
**Grated chocolate**

SERVINGS
8-10

# Bûche de Noël

Preheat oven to 375 degrees. Grease a 15½ x 10½ x 1-inch jelly-roll pan. Line with waxed paper and lightly grease again. Beat egg whites in a large bowl until soft peaks form. Beat in ¼ cup sugar, 2 tablespoons at a time. Beat egg yolks in a separate bowl and add remaining sugar, 2 tablespoons at a time. Beat mixture until very thick, about 4 minutes. Add cocoa, vanilla and salt and stir until smooth. Fold cocoa mixture into egg whites and spread evenly in prepared pan. Bake until cake springs back when gently pressed with fingertip, 15 minutes. Remove from oven and invert onto a tea towel dusted with confectioners' sugar. Carefully lift pan and immediately remove paper. Starting with long side, gently roll up cake and towel. Cool on a wire rack, seam side down, for 30 minutes.

Filling: Whip cream until it starts to thicken. Add remaining ingredients and beat until thick enough to hold firm peaks. Cover and chill. Unroll cake and spread filling to within one inch of edges. Roll up (without towel) and place seam side down on a serving platter.

Frosting: Combine sugar and milk in a saucepan. Bring to a boil, stirring constantly. Reduce heat and simmer for 6 minutes. Add chocolate, butter and vanilla and stir until smooth. Chill until frosting thickens, then beat to spreading consistency. Frost log and decorate with candied angelica or holly sprigs.

**CAKE:**
**6 eggs, separated**
**¾ cup granulated sugar, divided**
**⅓ cup cocoa powder**
**1½ teaspoons vanilla extract**
**Pinch of salt**
**Confectioners' sugar**

**FILLING:**
**1½ cups heavy cream**
**½ cup confectioners' sugar**
**¼ cup cocoa powder**
**2 teaspoons instant coffee granules**
**1 teaspoon vanilla extract**

**FROSTING:**
**1¼ cups granulated sugar**
**1 cup evaporated milk**
**5 ounces unsweetened chocolate, chopped**
**½ cup butter**
**1 teaspoon vanilla extract**

. . . let them eat cake.

*falsely attributed to Marie Antoinette*

SERVINGS
8

# Chocolate Cake with Rum Sauce

Preheat oven to 325 degrees. Butter and flour a 9-inch springform pan. Melt chocolate and butter. Stir until smooth. Cool to room temperature. In a large bowl beat eggs at high speed for 3 to 4 minutes. Gradually add sugar and beat until very thick, 5 minutes. Add vanilla, salt and cooled chocolate mixture and stir until smooth. Stir in flour. Pour into prepared pan and bake until a wooden toothpick inserted in center comes out clean, 30 to 35 minutes. Cool completely in pan on a wire rack.

Sauce: Combine cream, brown sugar and butter in a saucepan. Bring mixture to a boil over low heat, stirring frequently. Boil for 5 minutes, stirring occasionally. Remove from heat and stir in rum and vanilla. Spoon warm sauce onto individual dessert plates. Place a wedge of cake on each. Serve remaining sauce on the side.

2 ounces unsweetened chocolate
½ cup butter
2 eggs
1 cup granulated sugar
1 teaspoon vanilla extract
¼ teaspoon salt
½ cup all-purpose flour
SAUCE:
1 cup heavy cream
¾ cup packed light brown sugar
½ cup butter
3 tablespoons dark rum
½ teaspoon vanilla extract

**You should cook with spirits you would happily drink.**

*Julia Child*

SERVINGS
15

# Apple Cake with Caramel Sauce

Cake: Preheat oven to 350 degrees. Grease a 13 x 9-inch cake pan. Cream butter and sugar in a large bowl. Beat in eggs one at a time. Sift together dry ingredients and add to egg mixture alternately with apples. Stir in vanilla. Pour into prepared pan and bake for 40 to 50 minutes. Cool in pan for 5 minutes before cutting into squares. Serve warm.

Sauce: Combine all ingredients in a saucepan. Bring to a boil over medium heat, stirring constantly. Immediately remove from heat and spoon over individual servings of warm cake.

**Cake:**
**¾ cup butter**
**2 cups granulated sugar**
**2 eggs**
**2 cups all-purpose flour**
**2 teaspoons ground cinnamon**
**2 teaspoons baking soda**
**½ teaspoon ground nutmeg**
**½ teaspoon salt**
**4 cups peeled, finely chopped apples (Granny Smith or McIntosh)**
**1 teaspoon vanilla extract**

**Sauce:**
**¾ cup butter**
**¾ cup granulated sugar**
**¾ cup packed brown sugar**
**¾ cup heavy cream**
**1½ teaspoons vanilla extract**

SERVINGS
20

# Zucchini Spice Cake

Preheat oven to 300 degrees. Grease and flour a 13 x 9-inch cake pan. Sift together dry ingredients. Beat eggs in a large bowl until light and fluffy. Gradually add sugar and blend well. Stir in oil, vanilla, then zucchini. Blend in dry ingredients and pecans. Pour into prepared pan and bake until cake springs back when gently pressed with fingertip, 1¼ to 1½ hours. Frost cake when completely cool.

Frosting: Beat cream cheese and butter until smooth. Add sugar and beat until fluffy. Stir in vanilla.

3 cups all-purpose flour
2 teaspoons baking powder
1 teaspoon baking soda
1½ teaspoons ground cinnamon
1 teaspoon ground nutmeg
½ teaspoon ground cloves
½ teaspoon salt
4 eggs
3 cups granulated sugar
1½ cups vegetable oil
1 tablespoon vanilla extract
3 cups shredded zucchini
3 cups chopped pecans
FROSTING:
4 ounces cream cheese, softened
¼ cup butter, softened
3 cups sifted confectioners' sugar
1 teaspoon vanilla extract

SERVINGS
6

# Pine Nut Tart

Preheat oven to 375 degrees. Beat sugars, corn syrup, flour and eggs in a large bowl until smooth. Stir in vanilla, orange zest and pine nuts. Pour into prepared crust and bake until filling is almost set, 40 minutes. Cool for 1 hour. Melt chocolate and drizzle over top of tart. Spoon topping over individual servings.

Topping: Whip cream until it starts to thicken. Add sugar, cinnamon and vanilla and beat until thick enough to hold firm peaks.

⅓ cup granulated sugar
½ cup packed brown sugar
½ cup light corn syrup
1 tablespoon all-purpose flour
3 large eggs
1 teaspoon vanilla extract
2 teaspoons grated orange zest
1 cup pine nuts, toasted
Crust for 9-inch pie, baked
3 ounces semisweet chocolate
TOPPING:
1 cup heavy cream
2 tablespoons confectioners' sugar
1 teaspoon ground cinnamon
1 teaspoon vanilla extract

SERVINGS
6

# Warm Chocolate Tart

4 ounces bittersweet or semisweet chocolate
1½ ounces unsweetened chocolate
½ cup + 2 tablespoons unsalted butter
½ cup + 2 tablespoons granulated sugar
3 large eggs, room temperature
½ cup + 2 teaspoons all-purpose flour
1½ tablespoons cocoa powder
¾ teaspoon baking powder
¼ cup chopped pecans
Shaved chocolate for garnish
TOPPING:
1 cup heavy cream
¼ cup confectioners' sugar
1 teaspoon vanilla extract

Lightly butter six 1-cup soufflé dishes. Melt chocolates and stir until smooth. Add butter and sugar and stir until butter melts and sugar dissolves. Transfer to a large bowl. Stir in eggs, flour, cocoa and baking powder. Beat with an electric mixer until very thick, about 8 minutes. Stir in pecans and divide mixture among soufflé dishes. Cover with plastic wrap and freeze for at least 3 hours. Tarts may be frozen for up to 3 days before baking.

Preheat oven to 375 degrees. Remove plastic wrap and place soufflé dishes on baking sheet. Bake on center rack until edges are set and centers are moist and shiny, 10 to 12 minutes. Do not overbake. Cool for 10 minutes. Serve with topping (or vanilla ice cream) garnished with shaved chocolate.

Topping: Whip cream until it starts to thicken. Add sugar and vanilla and beat until thick enough to hold firm peaks.

Too few is as many as too many.

*Gertrude Stein*

SERVINGS 8

# TARTE TATIN

1 package (16 ounces) puff pastry dough, thawed
1½ cups granulated sugar
1 cup heavy cream
½ cup butter
3 medium Golden Delicious apples, peeled and sliced
3 medium Bosc pears, peeled and sliced

Butter eight 6-ounce ramekins. Roll out puff pastry and cut 8 circles the same size as ramekins. Melt sugar over medium heat until dissolved and caramel colored. Slowly add cream and butter. Mixture will ball up but continue stirring over medium heat until smooth. Pour sauce into bottom of prepared ramekins and layer with apples and pears. Top each tarte with a pastry circle. (May be covered with plastic wrap and chilled for up to 12 hours.)

Preheat oven to 400 degrees. Place ramekins on baking sheet and bake until pastry is puffed and golden brown, 20 minutes. Invert onto dessert plates and remove ramekins. Serve with Cinnamon Ice Cream (page 214) or vanilla ice cream.

SERVINGS 8

# BLUEBERRY SPRING TART

CRUST:
1 cup all-purpose flour
2 tablespoons granulated sugar
½ cup butter
1 tablespoon vinegar
FILLING:
6 cups fresh blueberries, divided
2 tablespoons all-purpose flour
½ cup granulated sugar
½ teaspoon ground cinnamon
TOPPING:
1 cup heavy cream
2 tablespoons confectioners' sugar
1 teaspoon vanilla extract

Crust: Preheat oven to 400 degrees. Blend flour, sugar, butter and vinegar in food processor until crumbly. Press mixture into bottom and two-thirds up the sides of a 9-inch springform pan.

Filling: Toss 3 cups blueberries with flour and spoon into crust. Combine sugar and cinnamon and sprinkle over berries. Bake for 1 hour. Remove from oven and immediately spoon remaining berries over tart. Cool completely before removing pan. Spoon topping over individual servings.

Topping: Whip cream until it starts to thicken. Add sugar and vanilla and beat until thick enough to hold firm peaks.

SERVINGS
10-12

# RASPBERRY GANACHE TART

Preheat oven to 375 degrees. Coat an 11-inch tart pan with nonstick cooking spray. In a large bowl, cream butter and sugar until light and fluffy. Beat in egg yolk, vanilla and almond extract. Stir in flour and almonds. Press dough into prepared pan. Prick with fork and bake until golden brown, 10 minutes. In a saucepan heat chocolate and cream just to a boil. Remove from heat and stir until smooth. Spread over crust and chill until firm.

Filling: Beat cream cheese and sugar until smooth. Stir in vanilla and amaretto. Spoon over chocolate layer and top with raspberries.

Glaze: Stir jelly over medium heat until melted. Boil for 30 seconds. Cool glaze slightly and brush over fruit. Sprinkle with almonds and chill.

CRUST:
½ cup butter, softened
½ cup granulated sugar
1 egg yolk
1 teaspoon vanilla extract
½ teaspoon almond extract
1½ cups all-purpose flour
¾ cup sliced almonds
1 cup semisweet chocolate chips
½ cup heavy cream

FILLING:
1 package (8 ounces) cream cheese, softened
2 tablespoons granulated sugar
1 teaspoon vanilla extract
2 tablespoons amaretto liqueur or ½ teaspoon almond extract
3 cups fresh raspberries or bing cherries, halved

GLAZE:
¼ cup red currant jelly
¼ cup sliced almonds, toasted

I generally avoid temptation unless I can't resist.

*Mae West*

SERVINGS
5 crusts

# PERFECT PIE CRUST

- 5 cups all-purpose flour, divided
- 2 tablespoons granulated sugar, divided
- 1 teaspoon salt, divided
- 1 cup lard or shortening, frozen in ½-inch pieces
- 1 cup butter, frozen in ½-inch pieces
- 1 large egg
- ½ cup ice water
- 1 tablespoon vinegar

Measure 2½ cups flour, 1 tablespoon sugar and ½ teaspoon salt into food processor fitted with a steel blade. Blend for 5 seconds. Add lard and pulse until mixture resembles coarse crumbs. Transfer mixture to a large bowl. Combine remaining flour, sugar and salt in food processor and blend for 5 seconds. Add butter and pulse until mixture resembles coarse crumbs. Add to lard mixture and blend well. Beat egg in a small bowl. Stir in ice water and vinegar. Add to flour mixture and stir until dough holds together in a ball. Do not overmix. Divide dough into five pieces. Flatten each piece onto plastic wrap making a 6-inch circle. Wrap tightly and chill for at least one hour before rolling.

*Pie crusts may be refrigerated for three days or frozen for three months.*

SERVINGS
8

# NUTMEG APPLE PIE

- 10 baking apples, peeled and sliced (12 cups)
- 1 cup granulated sugar
- 5 tablespoons all-purpose flour
- 2 to 3 teaspoons ground nutmeg, to taste
- Double crust for 9-inch pie, unbaked
- 2 tablespoons butter
- 1 egg, lightly beaten
- 1 tablespoon water
- 1 tablespoon granulated sugar
- ½ teaspoon ground cinnamon

Preheat oven to 350 degrees. Toss apples with sugar, flour and nutmeg. Let stand for 10 minutes. Line pie pan with bottom crust. Spread apples in pan and dot with butter. Cut decorative steam vents in top crust and layer over pie. Press crusts together, trim, then turn edge under and flute as desired. Mix together egg and water. Brush pie with egg wash. Combine sugar and cinnamon and sprinkle over top. Bake for 30 minutes, cover edges with a foil collar and return to oven until crust is golden, 40 to 50 minutes.

SERVINGS
8

# RASPBERRY PEACH PIE

1½ cups granulated sugar, divided
5 tablespoons cornstarch, divided
3 cups sliced fresh peaches, peeled and sliced
1 tablespoon lemon juice
½ teaspoon almond extract
3 cups fresh raspberries
Double crust for 9-inch pie, unbaked
2 tablespoons butter
2 teaspoons granulated sugar

Preheat oven to 425 degrees. In a medium bowl combine ¾ cup sugar with 2 tablespoons cornstarch. Add peaches and toss to coat. Stir in lemon juice and almond extract and set aside. Combine remaining sugar and cornstarch in a separate bowl and toss with raspberries. Line pie pan with bottom crust. Spread peaches in pan then spread raspberries over peaches. Dot with butter and lightly brush edge of crust with water. Cut decorative steam vents in top crust and lay over pie. Press crusts together, trim, then turn edge under and flute as desired. Sprinkle with sugar. Bake on lower rack for 10 minutes. Reduce heat to 350 degrees, move pie to center rack and bake until crust is golden and pie is bubbly, 45 minutes.

Good apple pies are a considerable part of our domestic happiness.

*Jane Austen*

SERVINGS 12

# Apple Raisin Crisp

Preheat oven to 350 degrees. Butter a 13 x 9-inch baking dish. Spread apple slices and raisins evenly in prepared dish. Combine sugar, flour, cinnamon and nutmeg in a medium bowl. Cut in butter until mixture resembles coarse crumbs. Sprinkle evenly over fruit and press down lightly. Bake until crisp, 45 minutes. Serve warm with vanilla ice cream.

**8 Granny Smith apples, peeled and sliced**
**¾ cup raisins**
**¾ cup packed brown sugar**
**1½ cups all-purpose flour**
**¾ teaspoon ground cinnamon**
**½ teaspoon ground nutmeg**
**¾ cup butter, softened**

SERVINGS 12

# Blackberry Cobbler

Preheat oven to 425 degrees. Butter a 13 x 9-inch baking dish. Spread blackberries in prepared dish. Combine sugar, flour and lemon zest and sprinkle over berries. Drizzle with lemon juice and dot with butter.

Crust: In a food processor combine flour, baking powder and salt. Add butter and shortening and blend until mixture resembles coarse crumbs. Transfer to a large bowl. Whisk milk and egg in a small bowl and stir into flour until mixture holds together in a ball. Turn dough onto a lightly floured surface and knead several times. Break off pieces of dough and flatten out to ¼-inch thickness. Place on top of berries. Repeat until entire surface is covered. Sprinkle top with sugar. Bake until cobbler is browned and bubbly, 20 minutes. Serve warm with vanilla ice cream.

**2 quarts fresh blackberries**
**½ cup granulated sugar**
**2 tablespoons all-purpose flour**
**Grated zest of ½ lemon**
**1 tablespoon lemon juice**
**1 tablespoon butter**
**Crust:**
**2 cups all-purpose flour**
**1 tablespoon baking powder**
**⅛ teaspoon salt**
**3 tablespoons butter**
**⅓ cup shortening**
**⅓ cup milk**
**1 egg**
**Granulated sugar**

SERVINGS
24

# CAPPUCCINO BROWNIES

2 tablespoons instant espresso powder
1 tablespoon boiling water
8 ounces bittersweet chocolate
¾ cup unsalted butter
1½ cups granulated sugar
2 teaspoons vanilla extract
4 large eggs
1 cup all-purpose flour
½ teaspoon salt
1 cup chopped walnuts

FROSTING:
6 tablespoons unsalted butter, softened
1 package (8 ounces) cream cheese, softened
1½ cups confectioners' sugar, sifted
1 teaspoon vanilla extract
1 teaspoon ground cinnamon

GLAZE:
1½ tablespoons instant espresso powder
1 tablespoon boiling water
6 ounces bittersweet chocolate
2 tablespoons unsalted butter
½ cup heavy cream

Preheat oven to 350 degrees. Grease and flour a 13 x 9-inch pan. Dissolve espresso powder in water. Melt chocolate and butter, add espresso mixture and stir until smooth. Cool until lukewarm. Stir in sugar and vanilla. Add eggs, one at a time and mix well. Add flour and salt and stir until just combined. Stir in walnuts. Spread mixture evenly in prepared pan. Bake on center rack until just done, 22 to 25 minutes. Center should be moist. Cool completely in pan on a wire rack.

Frosting: Cream butter and cream cheese until smooth. Add sugar and beat until fluffy. Stir in vanilla and cinnamon. Spread frosting evenly over brownie layer. Chill until frosting is set, 1 hour.

Glaze: Dissolve espresso powder in water. Combine espresso mixture with remaining ingredients in saucepan over low heat. Stir until smooth, then cool to room temperature. Spread glaze carefully over frosting layer. Cover and chill for at least 3 hours before cutting into squares. Serve chilled or at room temperature.

SERVINGS
40 pieces

# BAKLAVA

**PASTRY:**
1 pound pecans, finely chopped
½ pound almonds, finely chopped
1½ teaspoons ground cinnamon
¼ teaspoon ground nutmeg
¼ teaspoon ground cloves
⅓ cup granulated sugar
1½ pounds frozen phyllo dough, thawed
¾ pound unsalted butter, melted and kept warm

**SYRUP:**
2 cups granulated sugar
1 cup water
1 tablespoon lemon juice
1 thin lemon slice
½ cup honey

Pastry: Preheat oven to 350 degrees. Brush bottom and sides of an 18 x 12 x 1-inch pan with butter. In a large bowl combine nuts, spices and sugar. Set aside. Remove 8 sheets of phyllo and cover tightly with plastic wrap. Trim remaining sheets of phyllo to fit the pan. Cover tightly with plastic wrap.

Remove 4 of the untrimmed sheets. Place 1 sheet in pan and smooth it up the sides. Brush with melted butter. Repeat with the other 3 sheets. Remove 6 trimmed sheets, brush each with butter and place in bottom of pan. Sprinkle with one-sixth of the nuts. Remove 2 trimmed sheets, brush each with butter and place over nuts. Sprinkle with one-sixth of the nuts. Repeat process using 2 sheets at a time until all nuts are used. Brush any remaining trimmed sheets with butter and place over last layer of nuts. Butter remaining 4 untrimmed sheets and place over top of pan. Carefully tuck edges down the sides of pan.

Generously brush top with butter. Sprinkle about 10 drops of cold water over top to prevent curling during baking. Using a sharp pointed knife, score diamond shapes into top layer of phyllo. Bake until golden brown, 1 to 1½ hours.

Syrup: Combine sugar, water, lemon juice and lemon slice in a saucepan and bring to a boil. Reduce heat and simmer for 20 minutes. Remove from heat, discard lemon slice and stir in honey. Set aside to cool.

While baklava is hot pour half of the syrup evenly over top. Cool for 20 minutes then pour remaining syrup over top. Allow baklava to rest for 4 hours or overnight before cutting. Carefully cut with a sharp knife. Store at room temperature.

SERVINGS
5 dozen

# THUMBPRINT COOKIES

1 cup butter, softened
⅔ cup granulated sugar
1 egg
½ teaspoon vanilla extract
½ teaspoon almond extract
2½ cups sifted all-purpose flour
¼ teaspoon salt
½ cup jam or preserves

Cream butter and sugar in a large bowl until light and fluffy. Beat in egg, vanilla and almond extract. Add flour and salt and blend well. Chill for 1 hour.

Preheat oven to 350 degrees. Shape dough into 1-inch balls and place on greased baking sheet. Make impression with finger in center of each cookie and fill with ¼ teaspoon jam. Bake for 10 minutes and cool on a wire rack.

*Pecan halves or crushed pistachios may be substituted for jam.*

SERVINGS
4 dozen

# CHOCOLATE TIP COOKIES

1 cup butter, softened
½ cup confectioners' sugar, sifted
1 teaspoon vanilla extract
2 cups all-purpose flour
FROSTING:
1 cup (6 ounces) semisweet chocolate chips
1 tablespoon shortening
½ cup finely chopped pecans

Preheat oven to 350 degrees. Cream butter and sugar in a large bowl until light and fluffy. Stir in vanilla. Gradually add flour and mix well. Shape dough into 2½ x ½-inch fingers. Place on ungreased baking sheets. Using a fork, flatten three-fourths of each cookie lengthwise to ¼-inch thickness. Bake for 12 to 14 minutes. Cool on a wire rack.

Frosting: Melt chocolate and shortening. Stir until smooth. Dip unflattened end of each cookie into warm chocolate. Roll tip in pecans. Place on a wire rack until chocolate is firm.

SERVINGS
3 dozen

# HAZELNUT BISCOTTI

Preheat oven to 350 degrees. Butter and flour a large baking sheet. Combine flour, sugar, baking soda, baking powder, salt, cinnamon and cloves in a large bowl. Whisk espresso, milk, egg yolk and vanilla in a small bowl until well blended. Add to dry ingredients and beat until dough is formed. Stir in nuts and chocolate chips. Turn dough onto floured surface and knead several times. With floured hands, form dough into two 12 x 2-inch logs. Flatten tops slightly and place at least 3 inches apart on prepared pan. Bake on center rack for 35 minutes. Remove from oven and reduce heat to 300 degrees. Cool on baking sheet for 10 minutes. Cut diagonally into ¾-inch slices. Rearrange slices, cut sides down, and bake for 5 minutes. Remove from oven, turn cookies and bake an additional 5 minutes. Cool on a wire rack and store in an airtight container.

*Biscotti is a hard cookie, perfect for dipping into coffee or a fine dessert wine.*

**2 cups unbleached all-purpose flour**
**1 cup granulated sugar**
**½ teaspoon baking soda**
**½ teaspoon baking powder**
**½ teaspoon salt**
**½ teaspoon ground cinnamon**
**½ teaspoon ground cloves**
**½ tablespoon instant espresso powder**
**6 tablespoons milk**
**1 large egg yolk**
**1 teaspoon vanilla extract**
**¾ cup hazelnuts, toasted, skinned and coarsely chopped**
**½ cup (3 ounces) semisweet chocolate chips**

SERVINGS
4 dozen

# AMARETTO BISCOTTI

1 cup granulated sugar
1 cup butter, softened
3 large eggs
1 tablespoon amaretto liqueur
3 cups all-purpose flour
2 teaspoons baking powder
½ teaspoon ground cinnamon
¼ teaspoon salt
1 cup coarsely
chopped almonds

Preheat oven to 350 degrees. Grease two baking sheets. Cream sugar and butter in a large bowl until light and fluffy. Stir in eggs and amaretto. Combine dry ingredients, add to creamed mixture and mix well. Stir in almonds. With floured hands, divide dough into fourths. Shape each fourth into a log about 1 inch in diameter. Place two logs on each pan. Bake on center and top racks for 20 minutes. Switch pans after 10 minutes for even baking. Remove from oven and cut diagonally into ¾-inch slices. Rearrange slices, cut sides down, on pan and bake for 10 minutes, switching pans after 5 minutes. Remove from oven, turn cookies and bake an additional 10 minutes, switching pans after 5 minutes. Watch carefully to avoid excess browning. Cool on a wire rack and store in an airtight container.

Don't mess with us,
we haven't had our coffee.

*Joan Frank*

SERVINGS
4 dozen

# White Chocolate Macadamia Cookies

Preheat oven to 325 degrees. Cream margarine and sugars in a large bowl until light and fluffy. Beat in eggs and vanilla. Combine flour and salt and add to creamed mixture. Stir in macadamia nuts and white chocolate. Drop by rounded spoonfuls onto greased baking sheet. Bake for 15 minutes and cool on a wire rack.

- 1¼ cups margarine, softened
- 1 cup granulated sugar
- 1 cup packed light brown sugar
- 2 eggs
- 2 teaspoons vanilla extract
- 3 cups all-purpose flour
- ½ teaspoon salt
- 1½ cups chopped macadamia nuts
- 12 ounces white chocolate, chopped

SERVINGS
2 dozen

# Peanut Butter Cup Cookies

Preheat oven to 350 degrees. Combine flour, cocoa, baking soda and salt. Set aside. In a large bowl beat butter, peanut butter, sugars and vanilla until light and fluffy. Add eggs, one at a time, beating after each until thoroughly blended. Stir in dry ingredients until smooth. Stir in peanut butter cup pieces and chocolate chips. Spoon dough, 3 tablespoons per cookie, onto ungreased baking sheets. Bake until slightly firm to the touch, 13 to 15 minutes. Cool for 2 to 3 minutes on baking sheets. Transfer to a wire rack and cool completely.

- 2¼ cups all-purpose flour
- ⅓ cup cocoa powder
- 1 teaspoon baking soda
- ½ teaspoon salt
- 1 cup butter
- ¾ cup smooth peanut butter
- ¾ cup packed light brown sugar
- ¾ cup granulated sugar
- 1 teaspoon vanilla extract
- 2 large eggs
- 10 ounces peanut butter cups, coarsely chopped
- 1 cup (6 ounces) semisweet chocolate chips

SERVINGS
3 dozen

# Chocolate Ambrosia Cookies

Preheat oven to 375 degrees. Sift together flour, baking soda and salt and set aside. In a large bowl cream margarine, gradually add sugars and beat until light and fluffy. Add eggs, one at a time, beating after each until thoroughly blended. Stir in vanilla and orange extract. Add dry ingredients and mix well. Stir in chocolate chips, macadamia nuts and coconut. Drop by spoonfuls onto ungreased baking sheets. Bake until golden, 14 to 16 minutes. Cool on a wire rack.

**2¼ cups all-purpose flour**
**1 teaspoon baking soda**
**½ teaspoon salt**
**1 cup margarine**
**¾ cup granulated sugar**
**¾ cup packed brown sugar**
**2 eggs**
**1½ teaspoons vanilla extract**
**1 teaspoon orange extract**
**2 cups (12 ounces) milk chocolate chips**
**¾ cup chopped macadamia nuts**
**½ cup flaked coconut**

3 dozen

# Trail Mix Cookies

Preheat oven to 350 degrees. Coat baking sheet with nonstick cooking spray. Beat eggs until lemon-colored. Add oil and sugars and beat well. Sift together flour, baking soda and salt and gradually add to egg mixture. Stir in oats, wheat germ, walnuts, apricots and cranberries. (Dough will be very thick.) Drop by spoonfuls onto prepared pan. Bake for 10 to 12 minutes. Cool on a wire rack.

**2 eggs**
**1 cup vegetable oil**
**1 cup granulated sugar**
**1 cup packed brown sugar**
**1½ cups all-purpose flour**
**1 teaspoon baking soda**
**½ teaspoon salt**
**2 cups rolled oats**
**1 cup wheat germ**
**1 cup chopped walnuts**
**½ cup chopped dried apricots**
**½ cup dried cranberries**

SERVINGS
4-5 dozen

# THE ULTIMATE SUGAR COOKIE

Sift together flour, baking powder and salt. In a large bowl cream butter and sugar. Beat in eggs and vanilla. Gradually add dry ingredients and combine. Chill for at least 1 hour.

Preheat oven to 400 degrees. Remove half the dough from refrigerator and let stand at room temperature for 15 minutes. Lightly dust work surface with confectioners' sugar. Roll out dough to ¼-inch thickness. Cut with cookie cutters and place on greased baking sheets. Gather up scraps and chill. Repeat process using other half of dough. Combine scraps from both batches and repeat process. Bake until edges are lightly browned, 8 to 10 minutes. Cool on a wire rack. Decorate cookies with icing.

Icing: Combine all ingredients and beat until smooth. Add food coloring if desired.

**3½ cups all-purpose flour**
**1 teaspoon baking powder**
**½ teaspoon salt**
**1 cup butter, softened (no substitute)**
**1½ cups granulated sugar**
**2 eggs**
**2 teaspoons vanilla extract**
**Confectioners' sugar**
**ICING:**
**2 cups confectioners' sugar**
**2 to 4 tablespoons milk**
**½ teaspoon vanilla extract**
**Food coloring**

SERVINGS
20

# CRANBERRY TEA SQUARES

Preheat oven to 350 degrees. Grease and flour a 13 x 9-inch pan. Combine brown sugar, butter and flour. Pat mixture evenly into prepared pan. Bake until golden, 15 to 20 minutes.

Filling: Combine all ingredients and blend well. Pour over crust. Reduce heat to 325 degrees and bake for 20 minutes. Cool for 1 hour before icing.

Icing: Beat lemon juice, zest, butter and sugar until smooth. Spread over cranberry bars and sprinkle with pecans. Cool completely and cut into squares.

**½ cup packed brown sugar**
**¾ cup butter, softened**
**1½ cups all-purpose flour**
**FILLING:**
**2 eggs**
**¼ teaspoon salt**
**¼ teaspoon baking powder**
**1 cup granulated sugar**
**⅔ cup cranberry orange relish**
**ICING:**
**Juice and grated zest of 1 lemon**
**1 tablespoon butter**
**1¼ cups confectioners' sugar**
**1 cup chopped pecans, toasted**

SERVINGS
3 dozen

# Spicy Ginger Cutouts

½ cup margarine
½ cup packed dark brown sugar
½ cup molasses
1 egg
3 cups all-purpose flour
1½ teaspoons baking soda
½ teaspoon salt
2 teaspoons ground cinnamon
1½ teaspoons ground ginger
½ teaspoon ground cloves

ICING:

4½ cups confectioners' sugar
3 egg whites
¾ teaspoon cream of tartar
½ teaspoon vanilla extract
Food coloring

Preheat oven to 350 degrees. Grease baking sheet or line with parchment paper. In a large bowl cream margarine and sugar. Beat in molasses and egg. Sift together flour, baking soda, salt, cinnamon, ginger and cloves. Add dry ingredients to creamed mixture and blend. Cover and chill for 2 hours. Lightly dust work surface with flour and roll out dough to ¼-inch thickness. Cut with cookie cutters and place on prepared pan. Bake for 6 to 8 minutes. (Cookies should be just slighty baked.) Cool on baking sheet for 2 to 3 minutes then transfer to a rack to cool completely. Decorate cookies with icing.

Icing: Combine all ingredients in a large bowl and beat for 5 minutes. Add food coloring if desired.

*This darker cookie dough works well for gingerbread women, reindeer or leaf shaped cutouts.*

**He who laughs, lasts**

*Mary Pettibone Poole*

SERVINGS
6-8 tuiles

# Walnut Tuiles with Cinnamon Ice Cream

Preheat oven to 375 degrees. Butter two baking sheets. Combine brown sugar, corn syrup, butter and salt in a small saucepan and bring to a boil, stirring constantly. Remove from heat and stir in flour and walnuts until well combined. Spoon batter onto prepared pans 6 inches apart, using ¼ cup per tuile. Bake one sheet at a time on center rack until golden brown, 8 to 10 minutes. Cool on baking sheet for 2 minutes. Carefully remove each cookie with a metal spatula and drape over an inverted custard cup or tea cup. If tuile becomes too firm to remove from baking sheet, return to oven for a few seconds to soften. Allow to cool completely. (May be made one day ahead if stored in an airtight container.) Place on individual serving plates and fill with Cinnamon Ice Cream.

Cinnamon Ice Cream: Combine cream, milk and cinnamon sticks in a large saucepan and bring to a boil. Remove from heat, cover and let stand for 1 hour. In a large bowl whisk together egg yolks and sugar and set aside. Return cream mixture to heat and bring to a boil. Slowly add hot mixture to egg yolks, stirring constantly. Return mixture to saucepan and cook over medium heat, stirring constantly with a wooden spoon. Cook to 175 degrees on a candy thermometer or until mixture coats the spoon. Strain through a fine sieve into a bowl. Stir in vanilla and cool. Cover and chill for at least 6 hours or overnight. Stir in cinnamon. Freeze in an ice cream maker according to manufacturer's directions. Makes 1 quart.

**Tuiles:**
**¼ cup packed light brown sugar (no substitute)**
**2 tablespoons light corn syrup (no substitute)**
**3 tablespoons unsalted butter**
**¼ teaspoon salt**
**¼ cup all-purpose flour**
**¼ cup chopped walnuts, toasted**
**Cinnamon Ice Cream:**
**2 cups heavy cream**
**2 cups milk**
**4 cinnamon sticks, halved**
**8 egg yolks**
**⅔ cup granulated sugar**
**¾ teaspoon vanilla extract**
**1½ teaspoons ground cinnamon**

SERVINGS
8

# PUMPKIN CRÈME BRÛLÉE

- 6 egg yolks
- ⅓ cup granulated sugar
- 2 cups heavy cream
- 1 cup solid pack pumpkin
- 1 can (5 ounces) evaporated milk
- ¼ cup granulated sugar
- ½ teaspoon ground cinnamon
- ¼ teaspoon ground ginger
- ⅛ teaspoon ground cloves
- ½ cup packed brown sugar

Preheat oven to 300 degrees. In top of double boiler whisk together egg yolks and ⅓ cup sugar. Cook over simmering water, whisking until thickened. In a medium saucepan bring cream to a boil. Slowly add cream to egg yolks, whisking constantly. Continue cooking in double boiler until mixture is smooth and thickened. In a large mixing bowl combine pumpkin, evaporated milk, ¼ cup sugar, cinnamon, ginger and cloves. Pour hot custard mixture into pumpkin and stir until smooth. Pour into 8 custard cups (6 ounces each) and place in a large baking dish. Pour hot water 1 inch deep around custard cups and place in oven. Bake until custard is set in center, 50 minutes. Remove from oven and allow to cool for 30 minutes before removing from water. Cover and chill for 2 to 24 hours.

Preheat broiler. Force brown sugar through a sieve using the back of a spoon. Sprinkle 1 tablespoon sugar evenly over each custard and place on a baking sheet. Broil until sugar melts and caramelizes, 2 to 4 minutes. Serve immediately.

**As for butter versus margarine, I trust cows more than chemists.**

*Joan Gussow*

SERVINGS
6

# FLAN WITH EXOTIC FRUIT COMPOTE

Preheat oven to 300 degrees. Generously butter six 6-ounce ramekins or custard cups and place in a 13 x 9-inch pan. Whisk egg yolks until they begin to thicken. Stir in sugar and whisk until dissolved. Add cream and stir until blended. Pour into prepared ramekins. Pour hot water 1 inch deep around ramekins in pan. Bake for 50 to 60 minutes or until custard is set in center. Remove from oven and allow to cool for 1 hour before removing from water. Cover and chill for 2 to 24 hours. To serve, run knife around edge of each ramekin and invert onto serving plate. Spoon fruit compote around flan.

Fruit Compote: Bring sugar, water and vanilla bean to a boil. Stir until sugar dissolves. Remove from heat. Scrape seeds from inside vanilla bean into syrup and discard bean. Cool syrup. Combine fruit in a medium bowl. Pour over fruit and gently stir. Cover and chill for at least 1 hour.

**FLAN:**
**8 large egg yolks**
**½ cup granulated sugar**
**2 cups heavy cream, chilled**
**FRUIT COMPOTE:**
**½ cup granulated sugar**
**½ cup water**
**½ vanilla bean, split lengthwise**
**½ cup diced mango**
**½ cup diced papaya**
**½ cup diced pepino melon or sliced star fruit**
**½ cup diced kiwi**
**½ cup sliced strawberries**

SERVINGS
4

# LEMON MOUSSE WITH BLACKBERRY PURÉE

Beat egg yolks until thick. Stir in sugar, lemon juice and zest. Transfer to a double boiler and cook until thick, stirring constantly. Cool slightly then chill until almost set, about 30 minutes. Fold in egg whites and whipped cream. Spoon into stemmed glasses or brandy snifters and chill. Before serving, top with Blackberry Purée and garnish with mint.

Blackberry Purée: Purée berries in food processor, add sugar and blend. Strain purée through a sieve using back of a spoon. May be refrigerated for up to 5 days.

**LEMON MOUSSE:**
**4 egg yolks**
**½ cup granulated sugar**
**5 tablespoons lemon juice**
**2 teaspoons grated lemon zest**
**2 egg whites, stiffly beaten**
**½ cup heavy cream, whipped**
**Mint leaves for garnish**
**BLACKBERRY PURÉE:**
**12 ounces fresh blackberries**
**¼ cup confectioners' sugar**

Life itself is the proper binge.

*Julia Child*

SERVINGS
6-8

# CHILLED CHOCOLATE MOUSSE

Combine water and gelatin in a small bowl and set aside. In a saucepan stir melted chocolate and confectioners' sugar together. Slowly add hot milk, stirring constantly. Cook over low heat, stirring constantly until mixture almost boils. Remove from heat and add gelatin, sugar, salt and vanilla. Transfer to a large bowl and chill until mixture is slightly thickened, 45 minutes to an hour. Beat with an electric mixer until light and fluffy. Fold in whipped cream and spoon into a 2-quart soufflé dish. Chill for 2 to 3 hours. Garnish with fresh berries or chocolate curls.

3 tablespoons water
1 envelope (1 ounce) unflavored gelatin
3 ounces unsweetened chocolate, melted
½ cup confectioners' sugar
1 cup hot milk
¾ cup granulated sugar
¼ teaspoon salt
1 teaspoon vanilla extract
2 cups heavy cream, whipped
Fresh berries or chocolate curls for garnish

SERVINGS
8

# BERRY BERRY BAVARIAN

Purée strawberries in food processor. Combine gelatin with water in a saucepan. Stir constantly over low heat until gelatin is dissolved, about 5 minutes. Remove from heat and stir in sugar. Add puréed berries, lemon juice and vanilla. Chill until mixture thickens and holds its shape. Fold whipped cream into strawberry mixture. Pour into a 6-cup nonmetallic mold and chill until firm. Unmold onto chilled serving plate. Garnish with mint leaves and serve with Raspberry Sauce.

Raspberry Sauce: Pureé raspberries with lemon juice and water in food processor. Strain purée into a saucepan using back of spoon to remove seeds. Add sugar, bring to a boil and simmer for 15 minutes. Dissolve arrowroot in framboise and stir into raspberry mixture. Cool slightly. Cover and chill.

2 pints ripe strawberries
2 envelopes (1 ounce each) unflavored gelatin
1 cup cold water
1 cup granulated sugar
Juice of 1 lemon
1 teaspoon vanilla extract
2 cups heavy cream, whipped
Mint leaves for garnish

RASPBERRY SAUCE:
1 pint fresh raspberries
Juice of ½ lemon
¼ cup water
½ cup granulated sugar
½ teaspoon arrowroot
1 ounce framboise or kirsch liqueur

SERVINGS 16

# NEW YORK CHEESECAKE

Crust: Combine all ingredients. Press mixture into bottom and partly up sides of a 9-inch springform pan to form a crust. Chill in freezer until set, 5 to 10 minutes.

Filling: Preheat oven to 450 degrees. Beat cream cheese and sugar in a large mixing bowl until smooth. Add eggs, butter, cornstarch and vanilla and beat until just blended. Stir in sour cream. Pour mixture into prepared crust and bake for 1 hour and 10 minutes. When top becomes golden, cover with foil to prevent over-browning. Turn heat off. Allow cake to cool in oven for 3 hours with door slightly open. Chill for at least 12 hours. Serve with Raspberry Sauce (page 218) or Blackberry Purée (page 217).

**CRUST:**
- 1½ cups vanilla wafers, crumbled
- 5 tablespoons butter
- 1 teaspoon ground cinnamon

**FILLING:**
- 4 packages (8 ounces each) cream cheese, softened
- 1½ cups granulated sugar
- 6 eggs
- 6 tablespoons butter, softened
- 4 tablespoons cornstarch
- 1 tablespoon vanilla extract
- 2 cups sour cream

SERVINGS 16

# CHOCOLATE CHIP CHEESECAKE

Crust: Butter a 9-inch springform pan. Combine cookie crumbs and butter and blend until smooth. Press mixture into bottom of prepared pan and chill until set.

Filling: Preheat oven to 350 degrees. Beat cream cheese and sugar until smooth. Add sour cream, eggs and vanilla and mix until smooth. Stir in 1 cup chocolate chips. Pour mixture into prepared crust and sprinkle with remaining chocolate chips. Bake for 30 to 40 minutes. Turn heat off and allow cake to cool in oven for 1 hour with door closed. Chill for 3 to 4 hours.

**CRUST:**
- 18 chocolate wafers, crushed
- 2 tablespoons butter, softened

**FILLING:**
- 3 packages (8 ounces each) cream cheese, softened
- 1 cup granulated sugar
- 2 cups sour cream
- 3 large eggs
- 1 tablespoon vanilla extract
- 1½ cups (9 ounces) semisweet mini chocolate chips, divided

SERVINGS
16

# LET THEM EAT BREAD PUDDING

Preheat oven to 350 degrees. Butter a 13 x 9-inch baking dish. Tear bread into small pieces and place in a large bowl. Pour milk over bread and let stand for 15 minutes. In a separate bowl combine eggs, sugar, butter, vanilla, cinnamon and nutmeg. Stir into bread mixture. Add raisins, pecans and coconut and mix well. Pour into prepared dish and bake until top is golden brown and tip of knife inserted in center comes out clean, 1¼ hours. Serve warm.

Sauce: In a medium mixing bowl beat egg yolks and set aside. Melt butter over low heat and stir in sugar. Remove from heat and stir half the butter mixture into egg yolks, one tablespoon at a time. Stir egg mixture into remaining butter mixture and return to heat. Cook over low heat for 3 minutes. Do not boil. Remove from heat and slowly stir in bourbon to taste. Serve warm sauce over pudding.

**1 loaf (10 ounces) day-old French bread**
**4 cups milk**
**3 eggs, lightly beaten**
**1½ cups granulated sugar**
**½ cup butter, melted**
**1 tablespoon vanilla extract**
**1½ teaspoons ground cinnamon**
**1½ teaspoons ground nutmeg**
**1 cup raisins**
**½ cup chopped pecans**
**¾ cup flaked coconut (optional)**
**SAUCE:**
**3 egg yolks**
**¾ cup butter**
**2½ cups confectioners' sugar**
**½ cup bourbon**

SERVINGS

6

# Danish Christmas Pudding

Bring ½ cup water to boil. Add rice and butter and cook uncovered over medium heat until water is absorbed, stirring frequently. Stir in salt and milk. Cover and simmer over low heat until rice is tender and milk is absorbed. Dissolve gelatin in cold water. Stir into hot rice mixture to thicken. Add sugar and cool. Add rum, vanilla and almond extract. Stir in chopped almonds. Whip cream until it starts to thicken. Add confectioners' sugar and beat until thick enough to hold firm peaks. Fold in ¾ cup whipped cream. Add single almond to mixture and transfer to a glass serving bowl. Decorate with swirls of remaining whipped cream and maraschino cherries. Chill for 2 hours. Serve fruit sauce on the side.

Sauce: Drain fruit and reserve juice. Stir cornstarch into juice and cook over medium-low heat until thickened. Add jelly and carefully stir in fruit. Cover and chill.

*A single almond is hidden in the pudding to bring good luck to the finder.*

**½ cup water**
**½ cup white rice**
**2 tablespoons butter**
**¼ teaspoon salt**
**3 cups milk**
**1½ teaspoons unflavored gelatin**
**2 tablespoons cold water**
**⅔ cup granulated sugar**
**2 tablespoons rum**
**1 teaspoon vanilla extract**
**¼ teaspoon almond extract**
**2 tablespoons blanched almonds, chopped**
**1 cup heavy cream, whipped**
**2 tablespoons confectioners' sugar**
**1 whole blanched almond**
**Green and red maraschino cherries**
**SAUCE:**
**1 package (10 ounces) frozen raspberries or strawberries in syrup, thawed**
**1 tablespoon cornstarch**
**½ cup currant jelly**

I am beginning to learn that it is the sweet and simple things of life which are the real ones after all.

 *Laura Ingalls Wilder*

SERVINGS
8

# Frozen Yogurt Pie with Warm Chocolate Sauce

Preheat oven to 350 degrees. Combine wafers, butter and sugar. Press evenly into 10-inch deep-dish pie pan to form a crust. Bake for 10 minutes and cool. While crust is cooling, remove yogurt from freezer to soften. Fill cooled crust with yogurt. Cover and freeze overnight.

Meringue Topping: Preheat oven to 450 degrees. In a large bowl beat egg whites until stiff. Beat in marshmallow creme and vanilla. Spread mixture over pie, sealing to edges of crust. Swirl meringue into peaks. Place pie on wooden board and bake in upper half of oven until meringue has a few brown highlights, 3 minutes. Slice pie with a hot knife. Drizzle with Warm Chocolate Sauce and serve immediately.

Warm Chocolate Sauce: Melt butter and chocolate in a saucepan over low heat, stirring until smooth. In a small bowl combine cocoa, sugar, salt and milk. Slowly add cocoa mixture to chocolate mixture, stirring constantly. Bring to a boil, remove from heat and stir in vanilla. Serve sauce warm.

**28 chocolate wafers, crushed**
**¼ cup butter, melted**
**1 tablespoon granulated sugar**
**3 pints frozen yogurt or ice cream, softened**
**MERINGUE TOPPING:**
**3 egg whites**
**1 cup marshmallow creme**
**1 teaspoon vanilla extract**
**WARM CHOCOLATE SAUCE:**
**¼ cup butter**
**1 ounce unsweetened chocolate**
**⅓ cup cocoa powder**
**¾ cup granulated sugar**
**⅛ teaspoon salt**
**½ cup milk**
**1 teaspoon vanilla extract**

SERVINGS
8

# Ice Cream Soufflé with Fresh Berries

Stir ¼ cup Grand Marnier and crumbled cookies into ice cream. Fold whipped cream and almond extract into ice cream mixture. Cover and freeze.

Soften mixture in refrigerator for 30 minutes before serving. Reserve ½ cup berries for garnish. Combine berries, lemon juice, sugar and ¼ cup Grand Marnier and let stand for 20 minutes. Divide soufflé among eight goblets and garnish with berries and sliced almonds.

½ cup Grand Marnier liqueur, divided
8 amaretti cookies, crumbled
1 quart vanilla ice cream, softened
1 cup heavy cream, whipped
1 teaspoon almond extract
2 pints fresh berries (blueberries, blackberries, raspberries or sliced strawberries)
1 tablespoon lemon juice
¼ cup granulated sugar
¼ cup sliced almonds, toasted

SERVINGS
8

# Guiltless Grand Marnier Sauce

Combine milk, pudding, whipped topping, salt, Grand Marnier and orange zest in a medium bowl and mix well. Chill for 1 to 2 hours. Serve over fresh strawberries or raspberries. Top with almonds.

2 cups skim milk
1 package (3¾ ounces) sugar-free, instant vanilla pudding
1 cup frozen light whipped topping
⅛ teaspoon salt
¼ cup Grand Marnier liqueur
1 teaspoon grated orange zest
Fresh strawberries or raspberries
Slivered almonds, toasted

SERVINGS
2½ pounds

# ALMOND TOFFEE

1 cup butter (no substitute)
1⅓ cups granulated sugar
Pinch of salt
3 tablespoons water
1 tablespoon light corn syrup
1 cup coarsely chopped almonds, toasted
1 bar (4 ounces) milk chocolate
½ to ¾ cup finely chopped almonds, toasted

Generously butter a 15½ x 10½ x 1-inch jelly-roll pan. In a heavy pan over medium high heat cook butter, sugar, salt, water and corn syrup to hard crack stage (290 degrees) stirring constantly with a wooden spoon. Immediately remove from heat and stir in coarsely chopped almonds. Pour into prepared pan and spread mixture to edges. Cool for a few minutes. When cool enough to touch, remove from pan and place on a sheet of waxed paper. Microwave chocolate bar until melted. Spread over top of toffee and sprinkle with finely chopped almonds. Chill for 1 hour. Break into pieces and store in an airtight container.

*Both sides of toffee may be coated with chocolate, requiring an additional chocolate bar and ½ cup finely chopped almonds.*

SERVINGS
1 pound

# MICROWAVE PECAN BRITTLE

Lightly butter a large baking sheet. In a 1½-quart glass bowl combine sugar, corn syrup and salt. Microwave on high for 7 minutes, stirring after 4 minutes. Stir in butter, vanilla and pecans. Microwave on high for 1 minute. Add baking soda and gently stir until light and foamy. Quickly pour onto prepared baking sheet and spread thin. When cool, break into pieces and store in an airtight container.

**1 cup granulated sugar**
**½ cup light corn syrup**
**⅛ teaspoon salt**
**1 teaspoon butter**
**1 teaspoon vanilla extract**
**1 cup pecan halves or pieces**
**1 teaspoon baking soda**

I prefer Hostess fruit pies to pop-up toaster tarts because they don't require so much cooking.

NEFERTITI

# QUEEN OF GREAT TASTE

## "Love me, love my food."

Nefertiti. Now there was a woman who knew how to get attention. First of all, she was gorgeous. Second, she was the Queen of Egypt. ❖ Her name means "The beautiful lady." And she believed she was the most attractive woman in the civilized world. She worried that most Egyptians didn't know how to correctly pay homage to her beauty so she had her hubby the Pharaoh issue an edict to adore and admire her. ❖ Every Egyptian eagerly complied and Queen Nefertiti was very happy. Until she noticed that the diners at a royal banquet had the audacity to look at their food while they ate, instead of at her own pretty self. ❖ Her first reaction was to have all the guests banished to the pyramid-building crews. Then, she came up with a brilliant idea. She ordered all the tableware made in her image. That way, wherever anyone looked, there she was. Nefertiti goblets. Nefertiti platters. Nefertiti sorbet cups. ❖ Only one piece of Nefertitiware has survived antiquity. A beautiful, perfectly-preserved pudding bowl in the shape of her royal head. ❖ And, centuries later, we all still like a little extra attention when we put something special on the table.

Menus

# Mother's Day Brunch

## Appetizers
Caramel Brie with Fresh Fruit

## Breads & Brunches
Sausage or Chicken Crêpes
Basket of Assorted Muffins:
Am-I-Blue Berry
Apple Crisp
Raspberry Almond

## Vegetables & Side Dishes
Marinated Asparagus
Herbed Cherry Tomatoes

## Beverage
Orange Blush

# Patio Brunch

## Appetizers
Chili Bacon Grissini

## Soups & Salads
Gazpacho
Fresh Fruit with Poppy Seed Dressing

## Breads & Brunches
Queso Quiche with Avocado Salsa

## Vegetables & Side Dishes
Oven Roasted Red and Green Peppers

## Desserts
Pumpkin Crème Brûlée

## Beverage
Sangria Blanca

SERVINGS

12

# CHRISTENING BRUNCH

## SOUPS & SALADS

Tutti Frutti

## BREADS & BRUNCHES

Baked Crab Fondue

Tiny Cinns

Raspberry Cream Cheese Coffee Cake

## VEGETABLES & SIDE DISHES

Peas, Peas, Peas

## BEVERAGE

Orange Blush

20

# BABY SHOWER LUNCHEON

## APPETIZERS

Brie Wafers

## SOUPS & SALADS

Chilled Cucumber Soup

Cloisonné Salad

## BREADS & BRUNCHES

Chicken Triangles

Roma Cheese Soufflés

## DESSERTS

Kiwi Pavlova

## BEVERAGE

Prohibition Punch

SERVINGS
24

# Summer Salad Luncheon

## Soups & Salads
Carmen Miranda Chicken Salad
Shrimp Salad Caribe
Pasta Pecan Salad

## Breads & Brunches
Freedom Rolls

## Desserts
Raspberry Ganache Tart

## Beverage
Sangria Blanca

SERVINGS
12

# Committee Luncheon

## Entrées
Artichoke Chicken Casserole

## Soups & Salads
Regal Romaine
Spiced Peaches

## Breads & Brunches
Rolled Oat Rolls

## Desserts
Cappuccino Brownies

## Beverage
Iced raspberry tea

# Bridge Club Luncheon

## Entrées
Imperial Chicken with Madeira Mushrooms

## Soups & Salads
Marinated Asparagus

## Breads & Brunches
Tiny Cinns

## Vegetables & Side Dishes
Vermicelli Pilaf

## Desserts
Hazelnut Biscotti

## Beverage
Vanilla coffee

# Ladies' Tea

## Appetizers
Phyllo with Artichoke Filling

Curried Chicken Puffs

BLT Cherry Tomatoes

Alaskan Snow Peas

Zucchini Puffs

Fresh Cucumber Dip with Table Wafers

## Breads & Brunches
Poppy Seed Bread with Almond Glaze

Strawberries with Grand Marnier Crème

## Desserts
Baklava

Thumbprint Cookies

Chocolate Tip Cookies

Cranberry Tea Squares

## Beverage
Hot Tea

Golden Punch

SERVINGS 24

# Mediterranean Cocktails

## Appetizers

Aegean Salsa with Pita Crisps

Hummus

Phyllo with Feta Cheese Filling

Stuffed Grape Leaves with Chicken

Crostini with Tapenade

## Beverage

Pinot Grigio

SERVINGS 2

# Valentine Dinner

## Soups & Salads

Sweet Pepper Bisque

Field Greens with Goat Cheese & Walnuts

## Entrées

Veal à la Normande

## Vegetables & Side Dishes

Vermicelli Pilaf

Garlic Roasted Green Beans

## Desserts

Berry Berry Bavarian

## Beverage

Champagne

# Spanish Spring Supper

## Appetizers

Polenta Triangles with Peppers & Gorgonzola

## Soups & Salads

Sunflower Spinach Salad

## Breads & Brunches

Garlic Wedges

## Entrées

Spring Paella

## Desserts

Flan with Exotic Fruit Compote

## Beverage

Rioja

# River Festival Picnic

## Soups & Salads

Broccoli Raisin Salad

First Pick Potato Salad

## Breads & Brunches

Toasted Herb Bread

## Entrées

Cold Peppered Tenderloin with Tarragon Sauce

## Desserts

White Chocolate Macadamia Cookies

Peanut Butter Cup Cookies

## Beverage

Beaujolais

# Fourth of July

## Appetizers
Summer Quesadillas
Crostini with Tapenade

## Soups & Salads
Fresh Tomato Basil Salad

## Entrées
Pork Tenderloin with
Mustard Tarragon Sauce

## Vegetables & Side Dishes
Green Beans with New Potatoes

## Desserts
Ice Cream Soufflé with
Strawberries and Blueberries

## Beverage
White Zinfandel

SERVINGS
6

# Impromptu Summer Dinner

### in 45 minutes or less!

## Appetizers
Baja Nachos
Pretzel Pepper Dip

## Vegetables & Side Dishes
Santa Fe Sauté

## Soups & Salads
Spinach Cauliflower Toss

## Entrées
Grilled Salmon with Cucumber Dill Sauce

## Desserts
Blackberry Cobbler with Vanilla Ice Cream

## Beverage
Merlot

8

# SUMMER GRILL

## APPETIZERS

Crostini with Tomato &
Mint and Avocado &
Goat Cheese Toppings

## VEGETABLES & SIDE DISHES

Grilled Squash
Oven Roasted New Potatoes

## ENTRÉES

Lamb Chops with Mint Pesto

## SOUPS & SALADS

Fattouch

## DESSERTS

Lemon Mousse with Blackberry Purée

## BEVERAGE

Zinfandel

SERVINGS
16

# MEXICAN BUFFET

## APPETIZERS

Salsa del Mar with Lean Tortilla Chips
Frittata Baskets
Lavosh Tostada

## SOUPS & SALADS

Ensalada Cubano
Summer Celebration Salad

## ENTRÉES

Encredible Enchiladas or
Enchiladas con Pollo

## DESSERTS

Pine Nut Tart

## BEVERAGE

Sunset Sangria or Sangria Blanca

# Autumn Dinner

## Appetizers
Seven Spice Shrimp

## Soups & Salads
Salad Greens with Warm Brie Dressing

## Entrées
Garlic Roasted Chicken

## Vegetables & Side Dishes
Mashed Potatoes with Turnips

Broccoli Dijon

## Desserts
Chocolate Cake with Rum Sauce

## Beverage
Sauvignon Blanc

SERVINGS
2

# Hunters' Dinner

## Soups & Salads
Autumn Pumpkin Soup

## Entrées
Pheasant Marsala

## Vegetables & Side Dishes
Fruited Wild Rice Pilaf

Garlic Roasted Green Beans

## Desserts
Apple Cake with Caramel Sauce

## Beverage
Riesling

SERVINGS
8

# Anniversary Dinner Party

## Appetizers
Mushroom Walnut Pâté
Phyllo with Feta Cheese Filling

## Entrées
Seared Fillets with Shiitake Leek Sauce

## Soups & Salads
Spinach Watercress Potage
Mixed Greens with Sherry Vinaigrette

## Vegetables & Side Dishes
Potato Gratin with Boursin
Sweet & Savory Pepper Sauté

## Desserts
Tarte Tatin or Truffled Pears

## Beverage
Cabernet Sauvignon

SERVINGS
24

# Black Tie Buffet

## Entrées
Poached Salmon with Raspberry Sauce
Roasted Tenderloin

## Vegetables & Side Dishes
Vegetable Terrine
Asparagus Bundles
Almond Stuffed Zucchini
Citrus Rice
Potato Gratin with Boursin
Marinated Vegetables

## Soups & Salads
Cloisonné Salad
Fresh Fruit Tray

## Desserts
Chocolate Apricot Torte
Strawberry Marzipan Torte

## Beverages
Chardonnay and Merlot

# IMPROMPTU WINTER DINNER PARTY

## APPETIZERS

Zucchini Puffs

Crostini with Avocado & Goat Cheese

## SOUPS & SALADS

Sunflower Spinach Salad

## BREADS & BRUNCHES

Garlic Wedges

## ENTRÉES

Orecchiette del Mar

## DESSERTS

Almond Cake with Raspberries

## BEVERAGE

Sémillon

SERVINGS

4

# LET IT SNOW

## APPETIZERS

Spicy Artichoke Dip

## SOUPS & SALADS

Vegetable Lentil Soup

Salata

## BREADS & BRUNCHES

Peasant Bread

## DESSERTS

Nutmeg Apple Pie

with vanilla ice cream

## BEVERAGE

Chenin Blanc

# HOLIDAY DINNER

## SOUPS & SALADS

Wild Mushroom Bisque

Field Greens with Goat Cheese & Walnuts

## ENTRÉES

Crown Roast of Pork with Fennel Stuffing

## VEGETABLES & SIDE DISHES

Almond Stuffed Zucchini

Orange Glazed Carrots

## BREADS & BRUNCHES

Freedom Rolls

## DESSERTS

Bûche de Nöel or

Danish Christmas Pudding

## BEVERAGE

Pinot Noir

# NEW YEARS EVE

## APPETIZERS

Rolled Soufflé with Caviar

Sausage & Fennel Mushroom Caps

Gorgonzola Bites

Phyllo with Crab Filling

## SOUPS & SALADS

Mixed Greens with Sherry Vinaigrette

## ENTRÉES

Spinach Stuffed Salmon

## VEGETABLES & SIDE DISHES

Citrus Rice

Peas, Peas, Peas

## DESSERTS

Chocolate Bouchées with Créme Anglaise

## BEVERAGE

Champagne

## C

## D



## E

Could anyone fail
to be depressed by
a book he or she
has published?
Don't we always
outgrow them
the moment
the last page
has been written?

*Mary Ritter Beard*
*(endorsed by Candace Stultz & Sharol Rasberry)*

## W



## Z



HoHo® is a registered trademark of Continental Baking Company, St. Louis, MO

Bama Pies® is a registered trademark of Bama Pie Ltd., Tulsa, OK